Activism and Aid

'This book provides an insight into the thinking of a significant group of young Timorese women and men educated under the Indonesian occupation, who were active in the clandestine movement for independence. It describes how they promoted active citizenship immediately following independence through advocacy work and community organizing and how they dealt with issues relating to development and customary practice. I recommend this book to those looking for a perspective not often seen in the academic literature, that highlights the voice of those who themselves are affected by the policies of donors and international institutions. Significantly some of this generation are now coming into positions of influence in the country with the handover of the Prime Ministership from Xanana Gusmao to Dr Rui Araujo in February 2015.'

Dr Helen M Hill,
Honorary Fellow, College of Arts, Victoria University
(former Senior Lecturer Sociology and Community Development)
Advisor to the National University of Timor-Leste, Dili

Activism and Aid

Young Citizens' Experiences of Development and Democracy in Timor-Leste

Ann Wigglesworth

MONASH University Publishing

Monash University Publishing
Matheson Library and Information Services Building
40 Exhibition Walk, Monash University
Clayton, Victoria 3800, Australia
www.publishing.monash.edu
www.publishing.monash.edu/books/aa-9780980510874.html

Monash University Publishing brings to the world publications which advance the best traditions of humane and enlightened thought. Monash University Publishing titles pass through a rigorous process of independent peer review.

Design by Les Thomas

The cover photo shows the author with a team of staff and student researchers from UNTL, led by Community Development Department Director Abel dos Santos, when undertaking research in 2013. The team visited the memorial site of the Kraras Massacre in Viqueque District, where, during the occupation, all men and boys were rounded up and shot, and Kraras became known as the 'village of widows'. This visit was an emotional occasion for the students, some of whom had family members die there. They demonstrated their solidarity with the struggle with raised fists.

All photographs taken by the author, unless otherwise acknowledged.

The Monash Asia Series
Activism and Aid: Young Citizens' Experiences of Development and Democracy in Timor-Leste is published as part of the Monash Asia Series.

The Monash Asia Series comprises works that make a significant contribution to our understanding of one or more Asian nations or regions. The individual works that make up this multi-disciplinary series are selected on the basis of their contemporary relevance.

The Monash Asia Series of the Monash Asia Institute replaces Monash University's MAI Press imprint, which, from the early 1970s, has demonstrated this University's strong interest and expertise in Asian studies.

National Library of Australia Cataloguing-in-Publication entry:

Creator:	Wigglesworth, Ann, author.
Title:	Activism and aid : young citizens' experiences of development and democracy in Timor-Leste / Ann Wigglesworth.
ISBN:	9780980510874 (paperback)
Series:	Monash Asia series.
Subjects:	Economic assistance--Timor-Leste.
	Democracy--Timor-Leste.
	Timor-Leste--Politics and government--2002-
	Timor-Leste--Foreign relations.
Dewey Number:	338.95987

Printed in Australia by Griffin Press an Accredited ISO AS/NZS 14001:2004 Environmental Management System printer.

The paper this book is printed on is certified against the Forest Stewardship Council ® Standards. Griffin Press holds FSC chain of custody certification SGS-COC-005088. FSC promotes environmentally responsible, socially beneficial and economically viable management of the world's forests.

This book is dedicated to the Timorese activists whose passion and commitment to a free, independent and just Timor–Leste were the inspiration for this book.

ACKNOWLEDGEMENTS

This book was made possible by my ongoing connections with Timorese activist men and women whose passion, ideas and commitment to the independent nation of Timor-Leste were the inspiration for this book. Many of my original PhD research participants, as well as others, continued to share with me their hopes, dreams and disappointments as events unfolded in their newly independent country.

My deepest thanks go to the many young Timorese men and women who took part in my research; in particular I would like to thank Alberto Barros, Ergilio Vicente, Ego Lemos, Filomena dos Reis, Gizela da Carvalho, Laura Abrantes, Abel dos Santos, Jose Magno, Natalino Soares, Estanislau Martins, Alex Gusmao, Ismenio Martins, Nelia Menezes, and Vice-Minister Dulce Soares amongst many friends who shared their thoughts with me over the years, as well as many other original research participants with whom I have not been able to maintain contact.

I would also like to acknowledge the many friends who supported and encouraged me, including Drs Helen Hill and Russell Wright who supervised my PhD thesis, and Peter Taylor, my supervisor whilst a visiting fellow at the Institute of Development Studies at the University of Sussex. Also friends who read my manuscript, Allan Beesey, Christopher Sheppard, Dermot Clancy, Glenda Lasslett and Prof. Peter Kershaw whose comments on the book draft gave clarity to my thoughts.

CONTENTS

ACRONYMS

ADB	Asian Development Bank
AMP	*Aliança para Maioria Parlamentar* – Parliamentary Majority Alliance
APODETI	*Associação Popular Democràtica Timorense* – Timorese Popular Democratic Association
ASDT	*Associação Social Democràtica Timorense* – Timorese Social Democratic Association
BCTL	*Banco Central de Timor-Leste* – Central Bank of Timor-Leste
CAVR	*Comissão de Acolhimento, Verdade e Reconciliação* – Commission for Reception, Truth and Reconciliation in East Timor
CBO	Community Based Organisation
CEP	Community Empowerment Program (of the World Bank)
CSO	Civil Society Organisations
CPD-RDTL	Council for the Defence of RDTL
CNRT (1)/(CNRM)	*Conselho Nacional de Resistencia Timorense (Maubere)* – National Council of Timorese(Maubere) Resistance
CNRT (2)	*Congresso Nacional para a Reconstrução de Timor* – National Congress for the Reconstruction of Timor-Leste
CPLP	*Communidade dos Paises de Lingua Portuguesa* – Community of countries of the Portuguese language
DIT	Dili Institute of Technology
DV	Domestic Violence
EFA	Education for All
ETSSC	East Timor Student Solidarity Council
FALINTIL	*Forças Armadas de Liberação Nacional de Timor-Leste* – Armed forces for the Liberation of East Timor
FAO	Food and Agricultural Organisation
F-FDTL	*FALINTIL Forças da Defensa de Timor-Leste* – Defence Forces of Timor-Leste
FITUN	*Frente Iha Timor Unidos Nafatin* – Always United Front of Timor

FRETILIN	*Frente Revolucionària de Timor-Leste Independent* – Revolutionary Front for an independent East Timor
FKSH	*Feto iha Kbi'it Servico Hamutuk* – Young Women Working Together (formerly *Feto Ki'ik Servico Hamutuk*)
FOKUPERS	*Forum Kommunikasi Untuk Perempuan Timor Lorosa'e* – East Timor Women's Communication Forum
FONGTIL	NGO Forum
GDP	Gross domestic product
GFFTL	*Grupo Feto Foinsa'e Timor Lorosa'e* – Young Women's Group of Timor-Leste
HASATIL	*Hadomi Sustentabilidade Agricutura Timor Lorosa'e* – Love Sustainable Agriculture Timor-Leste
HDI	Human development index
IDPs	Internally displaced people
IOM	International Organisation of Migration
IFIs	International Financial Institutions
IMF	International Monetary Fund
IMPETTU	East Timor Students Association
INTERFET	International Force for East Timor (1999-2000)
KORK	*Klibur Oan Rai Klaren* martial arts group
KSI	*Kadalak Sulimutuk Institute* – Student Research Institute
INGO	International non-government organisation
LADV	Law Against Domestic Violence (passed 2010)
LDP	Local Development Program (of Ministry of State Administration)
MECYS	Ministry of Education, Culture, Youth and Sport (to 2005)
MoA	Ministry of Agriculture
MoH	Ministry of Health
MSATM	Ministry of State Administration and Territorial Management
MDGs	Millennium development goals
NDP	National development plan
NGO	Non-government organisation
OBJLATIL	*Organização Popular da Juventude Loriku Aswa'in de Timor-Leste* – The Popular Organisation of Timorese Youth Lorikeet Warriors
ODA	Official Development Assistance

OECD	Organisation for Economic Cooperation and Development
OJECTIL	*Organisação da Juventude e Estudentes Católica de Timor-Leste* – Organisation of East Timorese Catholic youth and students
OJETIL	*Organisação da Juventude e Estudentes de Timor-Leste* – Organisation of East Timorese Youth and Students.
OJT	*Organisação de Juventude Timorense* – Organisation of Timorese Youth
OMT	*Organisação da Mulher Timorense* – Organisation of Timorese Women
OPMT	Organisação Popular da Mulher Timorense – Popular Organisation of Timorese Women
PD	*Partido Democrático* – Democratic Party
PSHT	*Persaudaraan Setia Hati Terate* – (Lotus Faithful Heart Brotherhood) martial arts group
PERMATIL	Permaculture Timor Lorosa'e
POSKO	Coalition of Timorese NGOs for emergency response in 1999
PNTL	*Polícia Nacional de Timor-Leste* – National Police Force
RENETIL	*Resistência Nacional dos Estudentes de Timor-Leste* – National Resistance of Students of East Timor
RDTL	*República Democrática de Timor-Leste* – Democratic Republic of Timor-Leste
SSYS	Secretary of State for Youth and Sport
TFET	Trust Fund for East Timor
TNI	*Tentara Nasional Indonesia* – Indonesian Army
UDT	*União Democrática Timorense* – Timorese Democratic Union
UN	United Nations
UNAMET	United Nations Mission for East Timor
UNDP	United Nations Development Program
UNICEF	United Nations Children's Fund
UNTAET	UN Transitional Administration for East Timor
UNTIM	University of *Timor Timur* in Dili (until 1999)
UNTL	*Universidade Nacional de Timor-Leste* – National University of Timor-Leste
WHO	World Health Organisation

GLOSSARY

Tetun or Portuguese (p)

Adat (Indon. origen)	Custom
Aldeia (t)	Hamlet
Asimilados (p)	Timorese accepted as assimilated into 'civilised' Portuguese society
Bairro (p) *Bairu (t)*	Suburb
Bahasa Indonesia	Indonesian language
Barlake	Ritual exchange of goods between families at marriage
Chefe	Chief
Chega! (p)	'Enough!' (title of CAVR report)
Dato	Nobility, aid to the *Liurai* through Council of Elders
Ema	Person/s
Ema bo'ot	'Big people' – elders and seniors
Foho	Hills (rural areas)
Geração Foun (p) *Gerasaun Foun (t)*	'New' or young generation
Geração Milênio (p)	Millennium generation
Hamutuk Hari'i Futuru	The National Recovery Strategy in 2006 for the return and resettlement of the IDPs, stabilising security and strengthening communities
Juventude (t) *Joventude (p)*	Youth (plural) or young people

Lia nain	'Spokesperson' who has 'judicial authority' from the wisdom of the ancestors
Lisan	Traditional practices (law)
Liurai	King, traditional Timorese ruler
Lulik	Sacred
Loromuno	Timorese from western districts
Lorosa'e	Timorese from eastern districts
Mala'e	Foreigner
Maun bo'ot	'Big brother' (sometimes used to refer to Xanana Gusmão)
Maubere	Peasant (lit), used by FRETILIN to refer the Timorese people
Mesticos (p)	People of mixed blood
Pancasila (Indon)	Five guiding principles of the Indonesian constitution
Rede Feto	Women's network (name of women's NGO network)
Suco (p) Suku (t)	Village
Tais	Traditional cloth woven in Timor-Leste, worn by women as skirts and by men in ceremonial costume. Exchanged in *Barlake*
Tetun Tetum (p)	*Tetun Dili* is an official language of Timor-Leste. Derived from *Tetun Terik*, and creolised with Portuguese vocabulary.
Timor-Leste	East Timor after independence
Timorese	The people of Timor-Leste (excluding people of West Timor)
Uma lulik	Sacred house

MAP OF TIMOR-LESTE

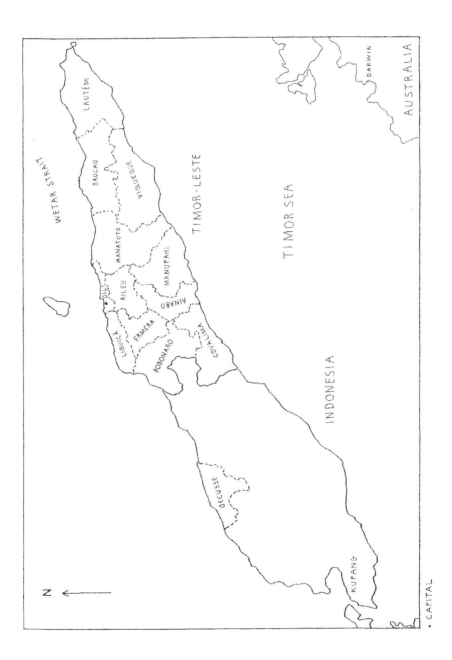

Filomena dos Reis is a key activist promoting peace in Timor-Leste and was awarded the N-Peace Award for peacebuilding work in Timor-Leste in 2011.

A Long Journey to Independence

We did not want to be slaves in our own land
We wanted to have self-rule
We wept and screamed for twenty-five years
Because we wanted self-determination
To rule ourselves
We, the women of Timor-Leste
Shed tears, wept and screamed
Because we wanted self-rule, to have self-rule
We did not want to be slaves in our own land
We stood! We stepped ahead
With courage and folded fist
We screamed louder!
Live or die, we wanted independence
We shed our blood
Flowing like a river
In every corner of Timor-Leste the women of Timor-Leste forgot their suffering
Because independence has now been accomplished.

Written by Filomena dos Reis, 8 October 1999

INTRODUCTION

The 'Young Generation' of Timor-Leste

Driving out of the capital Dili, the road rises sharply and we follow its tortuous route on appallingly degraded roads across the mountain spine of the mythological crocodile that is Timor-Leste. The 180 kilometre journey took some eight hours to reach Suai town on the southern coastal plain. It was the setting for a conversation with two Timorese activists, one driving and discussing animatedly with another about the situation of the younger generation Timorese and their hopes and dreams for the new nation. As student activists in the liberation struggle, they had channelled their passion for justice into civil society organisations. One had established the Covalima Youth Centre in Suai in remote Covalima district, while the other, originally from Suai, worked in an international non-government organisation (INGO) in Dili and later became a member of parliament. Like others in my research, these activists were still seeking ways to contribute to the development of their country, explained as follows:

> 'Youth of the liberation struggle now are looking for ways to contribute to development. We are continuing as leaders of youth organisations because we have the 'spirit of youth' to do something for our country'.[1]

Identifying as 'youth' because of their membership of the clandestine youth movement, they are known as the *gerasaun foun* meaning the 'young' or 'new' generation educated during the occupation in Indonesian institutions. The *gerasaun foun* does not refer to the youth of today, but to those born in the 1970s and 80s who, like 'Generation X', are a generation that gets older each year. The participants in this research were civil society activists who were educated in Indonesian institutions and had played an important role as student activists during the Indonesian occupation. By independence, most were in their early 30s, and engaged in the humanitarian aid programs that were being established by international agencies, or setting up their own civil society organisations.

Members of this generation have their own ideas about appropriate strategies for the development of their nation, which differ from those of the

---

1   Interview, Vicente, Suai, 7 August 2006.

older political leaders. Some describe themselves as the 'intellectual elite' of their generation. For them, citizenship of this new nation is a powerful motivating force; engaging in civil society organisations is a vehicle to contribute to the development of the new nation. The suffering endured by the Timorese during years of struggle provided the motivation and commitment for an independent East Timor[2] free from poverty and oppression, and the activism related to national development, is an extension of their long-standing struggle for national liberation.

The national leaders that established the key Timorese political parties in 1975 and continue in leadership positions today are from the Portuguese speaking '*1975 generation*'. Many of the Timorese political leadership lived overseas during the struggle, particularly in Mozambique and Australia.

The Timorese youth born after 1990 are distinguished by having graduated from the Timorese education system and have been described as the *gerasaun milênio* or the 'millennium generation' (Soares 2007).[3] They are too young to be bound to the ideals of the clandestine struggle, and have expectations of a better life than that of their parents.

These three generations are thus marked by different periods of Timorese history, resulting in learning in different education systems and facing very different life experiences. An activist from a student organisation in Dili explained:

> Our members are from the liberation struggle – they feel they are the 'lost generation' because of the choice of language. The government doesn't give any special attention for students who left education to be involved in the struggle and they feel abandoned. Even though Tetum is an official language, it is not used in the administration. The Government announcements say that Portuguese is the identity of Timor-Leste – this is the wrong story for Timor-Leste.[4]

That *gerasaun foun* continued to think of themselves as '*joventude*' (youth) perhaps reflects their continued role as activists and their felt exclusion from national government due to the language of administration which contributed to their sense of being 'a lost generation', 'marginalised' and

---

2   In this book the term 'East Timor' is used prior to independence and the Portuguese version of the name 'Timor-Leste' used for the post-independence era.

3   Dulce de Jesus Soares was at the time a Masters student at Victoria University in Melbourne, where I was also a doctoral candidate. From 2012, Dulce became Vice-Minister for Education in the 5th and 6th Constitutional Governments.

4   Interview Gusmão Soares, Dili, 29 July 2006.

'outsiders'[5]. Being raised in the heart of Timorese culture, many of them were the first of their families to gain an education, motivating them to be part of the process of overcoming poverty and oppression. Their ideas about appropriate development for the country embrace an allegiance to customary practices as well as a commitment to international standards of human rights.

Timorese activists interviewed in this research were influenced by the arrival of hundreds of English-speaking international agencies in 1999, becoming translators or establishing their own organisations to contribute to development in the lead up to nationhood. At that time a two-tier society emerged – the capital Dili, where resources were concentrated, rapidly westernised, while rural areas, with customary structures and way of life, remained largely unchanged. Sovereignty for the new nation of Timor-Leste was obtained on 20 May 2002, a day which officially marks the Restitution of Independence. The anniversary of the declaration of independence from Portugal on 28 November 1975 continues to be celebrated as Independence Day.

These development activists have often been critical of both the national leadership and of international aid agencies that have been influential in deciding the nation's trajectory and, as the 1975 political leaders move towards retirement, the alternative ideas, attitudes and perspectives of this next generation will become of increasing importance.

Citizenship and Active Citizens

Timor-Leste is a small half-island state sharing its westerly border with West Timor, part of Indonesia. However, one of its thirteen districts is Oecusse where the Portuguese first landed and which is now an enclave surrounded by West Timorese territory, only accessible from the capital by sea or air transport. Sandwiched between their giant neighbours of Indonesia and Australia, the formation of this new country is a story of tenacious struggle for self-determination in an entanglement of global politics, international aid and the lure of oil under the sea bed. For twenty-four years, from 1975 to 1999, Timor-Leste had been so isolated and abused that only minimal elements of an existing physical and administrative infrastructure were available to be drawn upon at independence. This first new nation of the new Millennium faced enormous challenges: not only were 70 percent of its buildings destroyed, but there were high levels of

---

5   Interviews with Gusmão Soares, Dili 29 July 2006; Vicente, Suai, 7 August 2006; Lemos, Dili, 11 August 2006.

poverty, low levels of literacy, a high fertility rate and 62.5 percent of its population under 25 years (NDS 2010). The international aid community played a major role in the process of conceptualising and building a new nation with the hope of transforming the lives of the people and helping them to overcome poverty. The first years of independence focussed on re-construction and establishment of institutions of state.

This book draws on the experiences of people of East Timor, who have been citizens of their own nation, the Democratic Republic of Timor-Leste (*Repùblica Democràtica de Timor-Leste* – RDTL), since just 2002. For the first time there was a national government which purportedly sought to understand Timorese culture and work to meet the needs of its citizens. What one could observe taking shape in Timor-Leste reflected a broader transition in development practice, in Timor-Leste as in Cambodia and elsewhere, 'international interveners' such as the United Nations and other international agencies were engaged in peace enforcement and nation-building activities through the implementation of 'democratic' models of governance and electoral processes as part of 'complex build-building operations' (Hughes 2009:1–2). Such processes in countries of Africa, Asia and Latin America are not new and indeed include Mozambique, which I myself experienced, as did the Timorese political leaders living there through the Indonesian occupation. In Timor-Leste, as power was transferred from the United Nations (UN) to a sovereign government, ideas of citizenship took place within diverse imaginings by the people and the international development industry. This book demonstrates, however, that development idealism of both political leaders of Timor-Leste and international development agencies was often out of touch with local realities and diverse aspirations and ambitions influenced the way of doing development and the way that one could be a citizen in this new democracy.

Citizenship as simply the formal membership of a nation state has been analysed and problematised so now it is considered that active citizenship must reflect the fact that rights and citizenship are attained through agency, and not simply bestowed by the state. It therefore includes social processes in which individuals and social groups engage in claiming, expanding or, in some cases, losing rights (Isin and Turner 2002; Gaventa 2006). Further, people's participation and agency in affairs that affect their communities are closely linked to the development of self-identity as a citizen (Kabeer 2005; Eyben and Ladbury 2006; Gaventa 2006). In general, political activism has been positioned as a critical and indispensable part of nation building. 'Active citizenship' is a relatively new contribution to the development lexicon. In particular, the development principle of people's 'participation' in issues and activities that affect them, is now well accepted but also subject to transformation as 'active citizenship' reframes the social meaning of 'participation' and places it in a framework centred around the notions of human rights and equality. As such, the dominant view to emerge is that people's participation in development needs to extend beyond participation in discrete activities to participation in the processes of state, enabling a sense of belonging as a citizen with rights and obligations. Active citizenship is supposed to enable people to participate in their *own* development, rather than that which is thrust upon them; it is supposed to encourage, rather than predetermine, the expression of their views pertaining to the official structures of state; it is supposed to make them 'agents of action' and 'advocates' for achieving human rights.

Not often is there a chance to study the first years of the development of a new nation, perhaps one reason that Timor-Leste attracts such attention. This book analyses Timor-Leste's first ten years of development through the experiences of younger citizens of the new nation state, examining their views with respect to the nation building process and their role within it. It also makes a critical assessment of the application of development knowledge and the role of international development agencies in this process. It explores the entangled nature of development theories, national economic development, civil society, gender and development, education and development, youth and conflict, and customary society and democracy. In each of these areas this book not only offers insights on the successes and failures of international development in the first ten years of Timor-Leste's existence, but also traces these processes of doing development bringing relevant lessons to diverse processes of post conflict development. It is important to distinguish between the process of state building, that put in place the physical and institutional structures of state, and nation-building which requires the establishment of shared values of its people (Harris and Goldsmith 2011:7). Much analysis of the state building processes has recognised the flaws in the top down processes but few have focussed on the bottom-up perspectives of a significant demographic of citizenry.

The focus of my study was the 'younger generation', but in the process of research the current day youth, termed the millennium generation by Soares (2007), became a new focus of concern in Timor-Leste, as a demographic 'youth bulge' resulted in large numbers of post-school youth facing an economic environment which had little capacity to offer them gainful employment. That Timor-Leste's population is extremely young is seen in table 1.

Table 1: Demographic Breakdown of the Generations. Source: (NDS 2010).

Generational group	Age range	% of population
Children	0–14 years	45.0
Millennium generation youth	15–24 years	17.5
'Gerasaun Foun'	25–44 years	20.0
Senior adults	45+	17.5
		100

A concentration on the technical tasks of state building in the early years eclipsed the needs and expectations of both former freedom fighters and a growing cohort of disengaged youth, arguably factors in the political-military crisis that broke out four years after independence in 2006. Just days before the political crisis broke out, the Country Director for the World Bank made an address stating:

> In these four years as an independent nation, Timor-Leste has been successful in maintaining peace and stability, a remarkable achievement, and an unusual one among post-conflict countries. This accomplishment is a tribute to the strength and commitment of Timor-Leste's leadership and the wisdom of its people[6].

The crisis which lasted from 2006 to 2008 was a wake-up call for both the Timorese leadership and the international community to realise that many of its citizens felt disregarded in the development process. It also resulted in an immediate shift of commentary from Timor-Leste as a major 'United Nations success story', to suggestions that it was a 'failed state', neither of which reflected the reality. These positions made a complex story simple and newsworthy for international consumption, but did little to explain the real tensions between the internationally promoted development taking place and the respective aspirations of the Timorese leadership, the rural population or younger generations.

This book promotes the concept of active citizenship as a means of engagement in the affairs of a state, including avenues of participation through civil society and governance processes. It employs the voices of younger generation activists to provide diverse perspectives which speak to those 'doing

---

6   Opening statement of World Bank Country Director for Timor-Leste, Zhu Xian, at Timor-Leste's Development Partners Meeting April 3-4 2006, Dili.

development' at the top, as well as drawing from the views of those purported to receive and benefit from the outcomes of development at the grassroots. Analysis of the perspectives of Timorese women's feminist struggle on the one hand, and the disengagement of the millennium generation of youth on the other, enrich the understanding of this complex society.

This case study of Timor-Leste demonstrates that governance processes based on Western democratic ideals can inadvertently create parallel systems to existing customary processes, based on different understanding, logic and principles of community values, rights and responsibilities. Citizens' participation and local understandings of appropriate development are principles of effective development, but development practice has too often failed to live up to these principles both in Timor-Leste and elsewhere.

Where development interventions are devised and brought in from outside without due consideration for local views, they sit alongside existing forms, rather than nurturing and developing existing knowledge and resources. 'Development' in Portuguese 'desenvolvimento' and Tetum 'dezenvolvimentu', means unravelling, opening the potential like a bud unfurling into a flower in full bloom. This describes development as something that starts from the potential that already exists at the core, a process by which new knowledge and resources can be absorbed to grow bigger, stronger, or in a new form. This book argues that participation in development, as it is theorised from development experience globally, provides a solid foundation for effective development. It also shows how in practice, a limited understanding and acceptance of the pre-existing culture can de-validate the voices of different groups in the society, resulting in development outcomes that fail to realise the potential that would be available if working in harmony with the existing cultural landscape.

The lessons from Timor-Leste's development experience are in some aspects similar to experiences in other post-conflict countries. Cambodia and Mozambique both faced complex peace-building interventions in which the UN and major international development agencies played a role in state-building and democratisation. The emergence of two-tier development in urban and rural areas is seen in small nation states such as Papua New Guinea and Solomon Islands where large numbers of youth face limited opportunities on leaving school and high levels of violence and entrenched gender inequality exist. The experiences of Timor-Leste are not unique, but as a newly emerging nation in the twenty-first century Timor-Leste is a unique case study.

Genesis and Synopsis of the Book

My first visit to East Timor was in 1997 during the Indonesian occupation. I was working with Caritas Australia as Senior Program Manager, and the fact that I spoke Portuguese due to my seven years living in Mozambique made me an obvious candidate for managing the East Timor program. I have worked in the NGO development sector for over twenty-five years with agencies such as Oxfam, Save the Children and International Women's Development Agency across southeast and south Asia, the Pacific, Latin America and Africa, including seven years living in Mozambique. My development work was interspersed by study, gaining an MA in Development Studies from Monash University in 1994 and a PhD from Victoria University in 2010. My doctoral research, which provides core material for this book, was carried out in mid-2006, just months after the worst of the violence had significantly changed the discourse about Timor-Leste's progress. From my original intention to focus on civil society initiatives there emerged a bigger picture, drawn from Timorese activists' perspectives that challenged the mainstream approach to development and democracy, resulting in my thesis 'Becoming Citizens: Civil society activism and social change in Timor-Leste', which was completed in 2009.

I visited Timor-Leste regularly for various assignments with international or Timorese NGOs which provided me a rich depth and breadth of engagement with Timorese civil society organisations. In addition, I undertook several research assignments which further contributed to the analysis in this book. A number of my activist friends also visited Melbourne for short or long term study, so I have been fortunate in being able to continue to engage with many activists whose perspectives inform this analysis, as they have continuously engaged in Timorese civil society to contribute to the development of their country. Their passion and commitment to a free, independent and just Timor-Leste was the inspiration for this book.

This introductory chapter is followed by an outline of the historical context of Timor-Leste's independence in chapter one. The occupation of East Timor over 450 years by Portuguese colonisers and twenty-four years of traumatic and contested Indonesian rule resulted in very different lived experiences for different generations of Timorese. The youth movement was central to the clandestine activities that supported the independence struggle. When humanitarian aid agencies arrived in 1999, Timorese students and activists became involved in international programs as interpreters, field workers and local partners.

The chapters that follow each focus on a thematic issue, underpinned by theory and the practice as experienced in Timor-Leste. Chapter two analyses the impact of humanitarian aid and the growth of local civil society organisations in post-conflict Timor-Leste. Civil society theory is used to analyse the humanitarian response and young people's participation in the transition, growth and transformation of Timorese civil society, which contributed to reconstruction and development in the county.

The roles of the international development institutions and how 'development' is understood is discussed in chapter three. The United Nations and the World Bank together played a major role in establishing the development trajectory of the new nation, but not without dissent from sections of the Timorese leadership and population. This chapter shows that some of the early decisions made about Timor-Leste's development failed to adequately involve the perspectives of the Timorese.

Customary practices which dictate the lives of the majority of the population are described in chapter four. Gender and development theory is used to analyse how customary roles constrain the participation of women and girls in activities outside the domestic sphere and how change can differently affect young men and young women. Meanwhile the women's civil society movement in the capital gives expression to women's perspectives concerning development and rights in Timor-Leste.

The impact of unequal development which drives urban migration by young people and the consequence of a large number of unemployed youth in the capital is considered in chapter five. The youth role in the political crisis of 2006–8 and its causes and consequences are presented, analysing the status of youth and culture of masculinities in the context of social change.

Chapter six analyses how the diverse educational experiences of different generations of Timorese impacted both on the quality of education and the self-identity of the participants. It analyses the kind of education required to facilitate rural development, build capacity to respond to existing conditions and enable young people to improve their quality of life.

Issues of people's participation in governance and development are analysed in chapter eight. People's access to governance and decision making is through the three layers of government, national, district/sub-district administrations and local Suco[7] councils. Recent research analyses the contribution of women and youth in local governance. The role of civil

---

7   The smallest administrative unit at the village level is the *Suco* (village) and the *aldeia* (hamlet). In the rural areas the Suco may be comprised of a number of dispersed hamlets. In Dili a Suco is comprised of several *bairros* (suburbs).

society in promoting community participation is also found to be critical in creating partnerships that best support effective aid-funded development.

The concluding chapter seeks to draw out some of the lessons from Timor-Leste's development trajectory and the influences that active citizenship can have on the development of the country. It highlights how inclusive development requires citizens' engagement and dialogue to build understanding between the new and the old, and a co-existence of international principles of individual rights and respect for indigenous practices. It is argued that civil society activists have contributed to bridging a gap in understanding between customary values and national policies which are being put in place. Younger generation Timorese will have increasing influence as more of them move into leadership positions but it remains to be seen how this next generation of decision makers will incorporate respect for Timorese culture while increasing equality of opportunity for women and girls in a maturing Timor-Leste. It concludes that development progress depends on citizens striving for change in a context where new pathways are open to them and donors recognise that mutual learning is needed to bring about effective, inclusive development.

Chapter One

ACTIVISM ACROSS GENERATIONS

When a development intervention takes place, whether big or small, the historical and cultural context in which it takes place will influence the outcome of the intervention. This chapter provides the contextual background to Timor-Leste's occupation by two successive powers and its struggle for independence, providing a critical understanding of the political, social and cultural environment which has affected the different generations of Timorese in specific ways.

The people of Timor-Leste emerged from years of war with resilience and a strong sense of independence as well as deep trauma from that struggle. Activism played a key role in Timorese history, the active front of the clandestine movement included Timorese youth and student organisations, the members of which have continued to play activist roles in the development of the new nation.

Portuguese Colonisation and 1975 Activists

The Portuguese arrived on the island of Timor in 1511. Initially their contact was limited to coastal trading missions, extracting sandalwood and other resources through treaty arrangements with local chiefs (Pinto and Jardine 1997). Overall, the Portuguese exerted little influence on Timorese society, establishing a permanent presence only in 1702, at the sandalwood port of Oecussi, now a district of Timor-Leste as an enclave surrounded by Indonesian West Timor. The Portuguese formed alliances with the customary chiefs of the coastal 'people of the sea' through whom they inserted themselves into the indigenous systems of exchange with mountain dwelling 'people of the land' to pursue their political and economic interests (Traube 1995). Only in the mid-nineteenth century did Portugal move to consolidate its hold over the country, imposing a regime of forced coffee cultivation in the highland areas. Coffee became a lucrative export, while the production of sandalwood declined due to overexploitation. Forced labour was used for road construction and a head tax was imposed to ensure agricultural production exceeded subsistence levels so that surpluses would be sold in the market (Pinto and Jardine 1997). The introduction of forced labour generated rising opposition to colonial rule.

Stirrings of nationalism were not evident until early in the twentieth century when a well organised rebellion by Dom Boaventura, the *Liurai* (king or traditional leader) of Manufahi, united almost all of the Timorese kingdoms (Babo-Soares 2003). In response, the Portuguese brought in troops, including some from Mozambique, to put down the rebellion, with huge cost of life. This 'pacification' of East Timor concluded in 1912, with Portugal effectively in control of the entire territory. Timorese society is made up of many different socio-linguistic groups, including those that traverse the border to West Timor. Depending on the classification of languages and dialects there are said to be from sixteen languages to thirty 'language varieties', while thirty-two languages were mentioned by respondents in the 2004 population census (Taylor-Leech 2012:58). Xanana Gusmão, hero of the resistance and first President of Timor-Leste, has suggested that it was Portuguese domination that generated the notion of common heritage between the diverse socio-linguistic groups of Timor-Leste (Gusmao 2000:102). The adoption of the Portuguese language at independence was a way to differentiate East Timor from West Timor.

Historically, the Portuguese administration did little to contribute to the infrastructural development of the country, or the well-being of their subjects. Formal education during the Portuguese colonial period was largely provided by a few missions of the Catholic Church. After 1941, the church was charged with the education system as an agent of the colonial administration, and for imparting Catholic and Portuguese cultural values to the traditional *liurai* leadership and other local elites (Molnar 2010:36). Those that had access to education under Portuguese colonialism were known as *assimilados*, that is, Timorese accepted as assimilated into 'civilised' Portuguese society, mostly sons of the *liurai* and *mesticos* (mixed blood). In response to popular protests about poor education and social welfare in 1959, the colonial administration began to increase the provision of primary education. Over the next ten years primary school student enrolment rose from 4,898 to 27,299 and secondary enrolments from 175 to 376 (Babo-Soares 2003:109). It is estimated that at the end of Portuguese rule no more than ten percent of the population were literate (Nicolai 2004).

In 1974 a bloodless military coup known as the 'Carnation Revolution' threw out the fascist dictatorship in Portugal, heralding a new progressive era. It was announced that colonial policies would be abandoned and independence would be granted to all Portuguese colonies (Ramos Horta 1987). The new democratic government took power in Portugal on 25 April 1975 and initiated a rapid process of decolonisation, despite the fact that no preparation had been made by the Portuguese towards local self-rule.

In East Timor political parties began to be formed by students returning from Portugal in 1975 with 'radical' new ideologies. As the beneficiaries of Portuguese education, the Timorese intellectual elite had been able to attend university in Lusophone countries, where they acquired knowledge of, and sympathy for, independence movements around the world, particularly in Lusophone Africa. Students from *Liurai* and elite families studying in Portugal established the first political parties – Timorese Social Democratic Association (*Associação Social Democrática Timorense* – ASDT) which was the precursor of the Revolutionary Front for Independent East Timor (*Frente Revolucionaria de Timor-Leste Independente* – FRETILIN) in 1974, as well as the National Democratic Union (*União Democrática Timorense* – UDT) and the APODETI party (*Associacão Popular Democratica Timorensa* or Timorese Popular Democratic Association) (Hill 2002:68–70). These three major political groupings were formed around different political aspirations. The nationalist anti-colonialist FRETILIN party wanted independence from Portugal. The UDT, representing the landowning and conservative elite, favoured remaining with Portugal with greater auto-nomy. The APODETI party had a small following of people that favoured local autonomy under Indonesian rule. According to Molnar, this party was led by the *liurai* of Atsabe, whose kingdom extended beyond both sides of the Timorese border and who sought unification of his people (Molnar 2010:44).

FRETILIN was founded by student activists in their twenties, largely people from middle-class families resident in the capital Dili. They did, however, have in their ranks representation from different parts of the country and so were not dominated by any particular linguistic grouping (Hill 2002:68). Members included Mari Alkatiri, the future first Prime Minister of Timor-Leste, and Jose Ramos Horta, the future first Minister of Foreign Affairs who became second Prime Minister, then President until 2012. Of his early involvement in FRETILIN, Ramos Horta later wrote: 'I had been named Minister for External Affairs and Information in the new, and first ever, cabinet of an independent, free East Timor. I was 25 years old, probably the youngest and least experienced cabinet minister in the world!' (Ramos Horta 1987:98).

An early coalition between FRETILIN and UDT had formed but collapsed some months later, due in part to meddling by Indonesia, resulting in a brief but violent civil war between them that left a legacy of bitterness to the present day (CAVR 2005).

FRETILIN declared the independence of East Timor on 28 November 1975. Rumours of an imminent Indonesian invasion had put pressure on these young leaders to act quickly. Following the invasion by Indonesia on 7 December, Ramos Horta was the diplomatic representative for East Timor from 1975–1999. For eight years, from 1976 to 1984, he was based in New York lobbying the UN. He was banned from entering Australia where other family members lived (Scott 2005). At independence he became the first Minister for Foreign Affairs, then briefly Prime Minister of an interim government in 2006, following a political crisis, and was elected as the second President on 9 April 2007.

Mari Alkatiri was born of a Timorese mother and Yemeni father who was a member of the small Muslim minority. He studied surveying in Angola, returning to Dili in 1975 to become co-founder of FRETILIN. Days before the invasion he was sent by FRETILIN to mobilise support for East Timor abroad. In Mozambique, he undertook a degree, graduating in law from the University of Eduardo Mondlane in Maputo. He remained in Mozambique as leader of the FRETILIN Political Front throughout the twenty-four year Indonesian occupation. He became the first Prime Minster in 2002 but was forced to step down in a political crisis in 2006.

The third major figure of the '1975 generation' leaders is Xanana Gusmão, popularly considered 'father of the nation'. He was the leader of FALINTIL in East Timor from 1980 until he was captured by the Indonesian military in 1992 and jailed, after which he led the youth movement of independence activists from jail. He was freed in 1999 and became the first President of Timor-Leste. Gusmão stepped down as President in order to form a separate party to contest FRETILIN in the national elections in 2007, and became Prime Minister, forming a multi-party alliance (AMP) following inconclusive elections. Gusmão became the Prime Minister of the Fourth Constitutional Government in August 2007 and was re-elected to lead the Fifth Constitutional Government in 2012.

The Indonesian Occupation and the 'new generation'

On 7 December 1975, just a few days after the declaration of independence, Indonesia invaded East Timor with tacit support from Australia and the USA. It was claimed that East Timor was not a viable state, due largely to Cold War fears in Indonesia and Australia about having a small left-leaning state on their doorstep. Australia did not oppose the Indonesian takeover of East Timor (Fernandes 2011). Indeed, on the strength of their tacit approval of the invasion, Australia negotiated a very favourable maritime boundary with Indonesia, in which it obtained access to the majority of the oil and gas reserves in the Timor Sea. Australia in 1978 gave *de jure* recognition to Indonesia's occupation of East Timor, becoming the only Western country to formally recognise East Timor as a legitimate part of Indonesia (Scott 2005). Indonesia's President Suharto was embraced as a cold war ally of Australia, the US and Great Britain, and these countries supplied military aid and technical assistance to the Indonesian military which was used against the Timorese. In spite of Australia's diplomatic efforts to persuade other nations to support Indonesia's position, East Timor continued to be an unresolved issue at the UN Security Council until 1999.

The Timorese armed resistance, FALINTIL, fought a bitter twenty-four year struggle against the superior might of Indonesia. Initially establishing *zonas libertadas* (liberated zones) in the mountainous areas, FRETILIN controlled over two-thirds of the population, as many abandoned their homes and sought refuge behind FRETILIN lines (Cox and Carey 1995:29). In the FRETILIN-controlled interior of the country there were disagreements on political ideology and violent purges against people who disagreed with the Marxist tendencies of some FRETILIN leaders or who wanted to surrender to the Indonesians to escape the hardship in the mountains (CAVR 2005:79).

Indonesia responded to the resistance with air strikes across the FRETILIN held mountain areas including bombing and chemical and biological warfare. The intensive bombing of the mountains by the Indonesian military in 1977–8 resulted in heavy losses such that the armed resistance of FALINTIL appeared to have been destroyed (Cox and Carey 1995). From 50,000 guerrillas in 1975, the numbers reduced to 700 by 1981 (Rei 2007). FRETILIN was forced to change its military strategy, sending much of the population down from the mountains to live in occupied East

Timor. The hardship faced by the people had been extreme. With limited opportunity to grow their own food in the mountains, starvation became another significant cause of death. By the end of the Indonesian occupation an estimated 200,000 people, a third of the population, had died (Pinto and Jardine 1997:106).

For the Timorese, Indonesia's most significant contribution to development in East Timor was to make education universally available for the first time. From the Indonesian perspective the education system was a way of influencing young Timorese. Students were expected to learn the *Pancasila*, the five guiding principles of the Indonesian constitution, and Indonesian national values, in 'an educational system designed to inculcate in children respect and admiration for Indonesia's values, beliefs and practices' (Arenas 1998). Rather than producing obedient Indonesian citizens, however, the system succeeded in breeding a new generation of independence activists. The use of education as a tool for instilling a sense of Indonesian citizenship failed, as Timorese youth and students became engaged in clandestine activities across the country.

There are two published accounts by Timorese activists of the underground resistance which I have chosen to draw on in this section. One is by former youth leader Constançio Pinto, who described the new era of school students beginning to support the resistance movement as it re-organised itself into small guerrilla units spread throughout the mountains (Pinto and Jardine 1997). The other is by Timorese activist Naldo Rei who, like Constançio Pinto, published a detailed account of his engagement in the clandestine struggle.

For some dozen years, East Timor was closed to the outside world, with Timorese living in complete isolation from the international community. It was only in 1989 that Indonesia finally declared East Timor open again to tourists and investors (Pinto and Jardine 1997). Meanwhile the Catholic Church played an important role in caring for the wives, widows and children of the freedom fighters and providing education. This also served to strengthen Portuguese as the language of the resistance, as well as giving leadership skills to youth which contributed to their later involvement in human rights advocacy.

The guerrilla force initially followed directives from the exiled FRETILIN Central Committee in Mozambique. But, unhappy with this situation, Xanana Gusmão broke with the FRETILIN leadership in 1986. There followed a reorganisation of FALANTIL and the formation of the united *Conselho Nacional de Resistência Maubere* (CNRM),[1] with Gusmão declared leader in 1988 (Niner 2009). Gusmão recognised that many pro-independence supporters were not FRETILIN members. National unity became an ideal of CNRM, in which the armed resistance, FALANTIL, was fighting for all Timorese, not only for the FRETILIN party. As noted, when Gusmão was captured by the Indonesian military, in November 1992, the armed resistance continued.

Timorese youth were engaged in the independence struggle, initially through the Organisation of Timorese Youth (*Organisação da Juventude Timorese* – OJT) which was tasked with supplying FALINTIL in the mountains (Ospina and Hohe 2002). In the late 1980s, as Commander of FALINTIL, Gusmão envisaged a new and distinct role for youth and students as the centre of the urban-based clandestine struggle (Nicholson 2001:19). From this point on, the Timorese students and youth organisations played a pivotal role in the secret movement, particularly through the National Resistance of East Timorese Students (RENETIL) led by Fernando de Araujo (known as Lasama), the Organisation of Catholic East Timorese Youth and Students (OJECTIL) led by Gregorio Saldanha, and the 'Always United Front of Timor' (FITUN) led by Armando da Silva. Through them, awareness was raised internationally about the human rights situation in Timor-Leste. Other organisations, such as *Orgão Oito*, led by Constâncio Pinto, operated clandestinely to directly support the armed resistance (Pinto and Jardine 1997; Nicholson 2001).

The first significant event organised by the youth resistance movement was for the visit of Pope John Paul II in October 1989. This visit was given great importance by the Timorese people, of whom over ninety percent became Catholic following the 1975 occupation.[2] Importantly for the history of struggle, the Timorese church was led by the Apostolic Administrator for East Timor rather than the Indonesian Catholic Bishops Conference. Thus East Timor, in the eyes of the Catholic Church, continued to be a separate country. This position was held by Bishop Belo for much of the

---

1   Conselho Nacional de Resistencia Maubere (CNRM). *Maubere* was a term of insult used by the Portuguese against the peasantry. It was adopted by FRETILIN as an endearing term for all Timorese people. In 1998 the name was changed to *Conselho Nacional de Resistencia Timorese* (National Council of Timorese Resistance).

2   The majority of Timorese had identified as Catholic only since the Indonesian census required them to nominate one of five official religions (Islam, Buddhism, Hinduism, Protestantism and Catholicism) and 98% ticked the Catholic box in the absence of an option for animism, the main belief system in East Timor (Timor-Leste Health and Demographic Survey, 2003, Dili).

occupation. He was initially accepted by the Indonesians as a 'moderate', but became sympathetic to and supportive to the Timorese struggle after he saw the human rights abuses perpetrated by the Indonesians.[3] During the occupation, the church gained increasing respect and acceptance by the Timorese for its role in providing sanctuary for independence activists being hunted by the Indonesian armed forces, and standing up for human rights.

The Indonesian authorities hoped the visit of the Pope would result in the Vatican recognising East Timor as part of Indonesia. The first demonstration of the youth movement was an action organised by the Catholic scouts aimed at overturning the possibility of this outcome (Pinto and Jardine 1997:110). The presence of contingents of news and media reporters for the Pope's visit was expected to ensure success in alerting the world to issues inside East Timor. A year later in 1990, another student demonstration took place during the visit of US Ambassador John Monjo. Students succeeded in entering the hotel where he was staying, presenting flowers and a petition and talking directly with him. Many of the demonstrators were afterwards severely beaten by the Indonesian armed forces (Pinto and Jardine 1997:117). These student actions drew international attention to the situation prevailing in East Timor, for the first time in more than a dozen years.

In 1991 a Portuguese parliamentary delegation was planning to visit the territory which, it was hoped, would resolve the status of East Timor.[4] Student activists, led by the Organisation of Youth and Students of Timor-Leste (*Organização Juventude Estudante de Timor-Leste* – OJETIL),[5] had been planning for the visit for a year, but it was cancelled. The military started hunting down student activists and many students sought protection by hiding in Motael church (Pinto and Jardine 1997:182). The Indonesians surrounded the church, shot and killed one of the student activists – Sabastião Gomes – and arrested twenty-five others.

Sabastião Gomes' funeral became a symbol of resistance. Several thousand, mostly young people, joined the procession to the cemetery. Fully

---

3   I worked as East Timor Program Manager for the Catholic organisation Caritas Australia from 1997 to 2000. I refer here to what I learned during that period working in partnership with Caritas Dili which was intimately involved in human rights issues.

4   Beginning in 1982, at the request of the General Assembly, successive Secretaries-General (SG) held regular talks with Indonesia and Portugal aimed at resolving the status of the territory.

5   OJETIL was a major Fretilin youth organisation formed in the 1990s from the Catholic youth organisation OJECTIL.

armed Indonesian troops opened fire on the young mourners, killing 271 students and youth and injuring hundreds more (Pinto 2001). This event in November 1991 became known as the Santa Cruz Massacre and was a pivotal moment for the resistance struggle. The presence of Western photographers and film makers at the event helped inform the world of the atrocities taking place in East Timor.[6]

Statue commemorating the 12 November Santa Cruz massacre
where 271 youth were killed.

In the wake of the Santa Cruz massacre, the leadership gave a new prominence to the student and youth movements' crucial role in the pursuit of Timorese independence. To complement the Political Front led by Mari Alkatiri in Mozambique and the Diplomatic Front led by Jose Ramos Horta in Australia and the US, a Clandestine Front was established involving four youth organisations in East Timor and Indonesia. From then, according to Pinto, the resistance was in the hands of the new generation (Pinto and Jardine 1997:237–8).

Timorese activist Naldo Rei describes the high degree of intercommunication between Xanana Gusmão, as the leader of FALINTIL, and the clandestine youth movement. For example Rei received direct communication

6   These include photographer Peter Cox, who with writer Peter Carey, published a book 'Generations of Resistance in East Timor' on the youth movement, and film maker Max Stahl, a British television journalist who produced a documentary 'Cold Blood' on the Santa Cruz massacre.

from Xanana telling him to organise a demonstration in Dili to coincide with a meeting with non-aligned world leaders in Jakarta in 1992 (Rei 2007:60).

The student movement broadened its scope on two fronts from 1992. RENETIL, the clandestine organisation for Timorese students studying in Indonesia, began collaborating with Indonesian student organisations to inform and engage Indonesian students in the Timorese struggle. As well, the movement expanded its focus from the liberation struggle to other issues of human rights and democracy within Indonesia. Significantly, this resulted in demonstrations for the Timorese struggle being held in Jakarta. For instance on 7 December 1995, the twentieth anniversary of the Indonesian invasion, the Timorese students scaled the fences of the Dutch and Russian embassies in Jakarta, demanding self-determination via a referendum (Sword Gusmao 2003; Rei 2007). Timorese student activism is said to have played no small part in the pro-democracy movement which eventually toppled Suharto from power on 21 May 1998 (Nicholson 2001).

Outside East Timor RENETIL members were able to meet and have discussions more freely, including with students from other islands of Indonesia, politicising them in issues of democracy and freedom.[7] The official Indonesian East Timor Students Association, IMPETTU,[8] was infiltrated by RENETIL members to convert it into a pro-independence organisation supporting the clandestine movement.[9]

Within East Timor, young people were engaged in the resistance movement through a network of small pro-independence groups. Different youth or women's cells were responsible for providing medical supplies and food to particular groups of resistance fighters in the mountains (Pinto and Jardine 1997). Others sold goods to raise funds for the resistance. Each clandestine cell had a code name and would work without knowledge of what other cells were doing to keep the identity of members of the pro-independence movement secure (Pinto and Jardine 1997). Students with knowledge of English played an important role in developing contacts to pass information from the resistance leadership out of the country. Others in Jakarta were couriers and disseminators of documents from the resistance guerrillas (Sword Gusmao 2003).

---

7   Interview, Samala Rua, Dili, 31 July 2006.
8   IMPETTU – *Ikatan Mahasiswa Pelajar Timor Timur.*
9   The politicisation of IMPETTU had been a strategy of RENETIL since its inception. In Denpasar, the birthplace of RENETIL, all IMPETTU leaders after 1989 were RENETIL members. Student leaders were able to use IMPETTU to organise allowable student events which RENETIL, as a clandestine organisation, used as cover for more subversive activities.

The Catholic Church also played a role in organising youth and many churches and missions become safe havens for targeted pro-independence youth. The Catholic youth groups such as Catholic Scouts became an important forum for analysis and reflection about the violence that was taking place in the community, and was also one of the few youth organisations which encouraged girls' participation.[10]

There were, however, also youth who joined the Indonesian intelligence organisations and the military fuelled inter-communal conflict by promoting and funding youth gangs such as the *Ninjas, Gadapaksi*. The *Ninjas* emerged in Dili in 1995 roaming the streets at night, intimidating and kidnapping independence supporters. The *Gadapaksi* (Youth Front for Upholding *Pancasila*) emerged a year later, provoking disturbances among the Timorese by instigating fights with Catholic youth. In 1997 and 1998, Caritas Dili staff referred to provocations such as Gadapaksi members insulting Bishops or priests and disrupting Catholic ceremonies.[11] Like the *Ninjas* they were drawn from unemployed East Timorese youth and were linked to criminal networks and the Indonesian Special Forces.[12] *Gadapaksi* were paid a monthly stipend by the Indonesian military. The *Gadapaksi* youth informed the military about pro-independence youth who would then be kidnapped in night time raids. These tactics helped to create an impression that internal divisions were at the heart of the 'Timor problem'.

Despite Indonesian oppression and intimidation, the UNTIM students found they were able to voice community concerns as a student body from within the university. One activist described how people from the community came to the university to complain of being intimidated by the Indonesian military and to ask the students to inform the civilian authorities. Students would raise the issues with the government and, if there was no response, they would hold a demonstration. The first demonstration following the 1991 Santa Cruz massacre was in July 1994, but after that demonstrations were held regularly by UNTIM students.[13]

President Suharto's downfall in May 1998 was a turning point for East Timor: political expression and organisation was permitted for the first time since 1975. In Jakarta, Indonesian students demonstrated and spoke openly

---

10   Interview Abrantes, Dili, 30 July 2006.
11   I worked as East Timor Program Manager for Caritas Australia from 1997–2000, and regularly visited East Timor during that period, working in partnership with Caritas Dili.
12   James Scambary – personal communication 8th July 2008. The Special Forces are known as *Kopassus.*
13   Interview Barros, Suai, 7 August 2006.

to the press about the injustices that President Suharto had perpetrated against the people. The Timorese instantly recognised this was a new period of political openness, which gave rise to new hope within Timor.[14] In the months that followed, groups of people started to congregate in the streets, discussing or socialising, something unheard of previously as it had been forbidden for more than four people to meet except at Catholic Mass.

UNTIM students in Dili held a meeting in June 1998 with 500 students, forming the East Timor Student Solidarity Council (ETSSC), known in Indonesian as *Dewan Solidaritas Mahasiswa*. ETSSC had a new socio-political mission focussed on issues pertaining to peace, democracy, reconciliation, and the promotion of self-determination through a referendum.[15] In June 1998, ETSSC initiated a series of rallies at UNTIM in Dili calling for an end to human rights violations and demanding a referendum and an end to the military occupation (ETAN 2000).

On 9 June 1998 Suharto's successor, President Habibie, suggested that he would be willing to grant East Timor 'special autonomy' in exchange for Timorese recognition of Indonesian sovereignty (Lloyd 2000). This offer was rejected by the Timorese, but it paved the way for the United Nations (UN) to initiate a transition plan (Smillie and Minear 2004:61). Following this, the students travelled to every district and sub-district to hold dialogues to help the people understand their democratic rights, to understand what a referendum would mean and invite them to express their views on the future of the country (Taudevin 1999:185–6).

Arrival of the UN and International Agencies

In early 1999 President Habibie announced that the East Timorese would be given the opportunity to decide on their future through popular consultation. On 5 May 1999 an agreement between Indonesia, Portugal and the UN was signed in New York – the culmination of seventeen years of negotiations by the offices of the UN Secretary –General (Martin 2000). The agreement outlined the principles for a universal popular consultation, a secret ballot by which the Timorese could vote for or against autonomy

---

14   Personal observation during visits to East Timor in 1997-8 as Program Manager for
       Caritas Australia. At a meeting held in Bali with my Caritas Dili colleagues (because
       it was unsafe for them to hold a meeting with foreigners in Dili) we watched reports
       of Suharto's downfall on Indonesian television. My colleagues were amazed and
       excited to hear interviews of rebellious Javanese youth being broadcast on TV, the first
       time they heard alternative opinions to the government line expressed in the media.
15   Interview, Gusmão Soares, Dili, 29 July 2006.

within Indonesia. If they rejected autonomy there would be a transfer of authority through the UN to independence. This paved the way for UN Security Council Resolution 1246 to establish a United Nations Assistance Mission in East Timor (UNAMET) which would set in place conditions for a UN sponsored popular consultation on autonomy. A condition imposed by Indonesia was that they alone would be responsible for the security arrangements (DFAT 2001).

A new wave of attacks against independence supporters across the country had already started with killings in Alas in late 1998. From this time, Timorese youth were being recruited into locally based militia that were provided with arms and monthly stipends by the Indonesian military to guarantee their willingness to carry out acts of violence on command. Sporadic unprovoked attacks on pro-independence communities involved vicious killings and widespread burning of houses. The trickle of people who fled their villages in January became a steady stream. At the end of January 1999 there were 5,000 internally displaced people (IDPs). The reign of terror in the countryside resulted in numbers of IDPs escalating to 60,000 by July (Smillie and Minear 2004). The horrific events which led to this displacement are presented in a journalist's detailed account (Martinkus 2001).

The political situation continued to deteriorate. The ETSSC forums could no longer be held as ETSSC students were targeted. The District Co-ordinator of ETSSC in Covalima explained: 'Militia from Mahidi and Laksaur tried to kill me many times. They came to my house in the day and in the night. Then one day the Commander of the TNI (Indonesian army) came to my house with weapons. I managed to escape'.[16] He was forced to flee to Kupang in West Timor in April 1999 and did not return until July when he was called to assist the registration of voters for the independence ballot.

Fear amongst the Timorese was understandably high – there were few international observers and the UN personnel did not start arriving until late May to prepare for the ballot in August. In Liquiça Church in April 1999 over one hundred people seeking refuge from the militia were massacred. This took place when many Timorese scholars and activists were in Melbourne for a Timorese Development Planning Conference organised by the National Council of Timorese Resistance (CNRT) in Melbourne. On hearing of the massacre the participants were devastated; a number lost family members. Caritas Australia, which had supported the Director of Caritas Dili to attend the conference, made arrangements for him to meet

---

16   Interview, Vicente, Suai 7 August 2006.

A student activist and member of ETSSC at university in Dili, Ergilio Ferreira Vicente founded the Suai Youth Centre and continued as Coordinator for many years. The banner reads, 'Build capacity, Create ideas, Nurture creativity and Strengthen unity'. Ergilio now coordinates the Youth Parliament Program for the Secretary of Youth and Sport in Dili.

Foreign Minister Alexander Downer to provide an eyewitness account of the violence that was unfolding inside the country. Disappointingly, the Foreign Minister maintained the official Australian view that 'rogue elements' were responsible for the violence, even though witnesses in East Timor reported that the Indonesian military was instigating the violence.[17]

---

17   I attended the meeting and acted as translator from Portuguese.

Following this, Caritas Australia sought Timorese views about how it could help. Father Barreto, the Director of Caritas Dili, had no hesitation in his response – he asked for international witnesses to come to Timor to act as a deterrent to the violence that was being unleashed against the Timorese people. A Caritas volunteer 'witness program' was quickly devised, which I coordinated, resulting in a dozen religious sisters, health workers and Australian resident Timorese volunteering to work alongside Timorese colleagues in church organisations or clinics, protecting them with their simple presence as foreign observers. Once the UN volunteers arrived to assist the ballot in May and June they also played an important role in this regard.

UNAMET set up operations in May 1999 with over 400 foreign UN volunteers making up the corps of electoral officers, assisted by 600 local Timorese staff (DFAT 2001:93). Timorese students who were studying in Indonesia returned to help enrol voters for the ballot. Educated young people who had learned some English were employed by UNAMET as interpreters. This sudden and massive requirement for interpreters and translators catapulted large numbers of young Timorese into a new context of foreign values and the English language medium of communication. This opened new opportunities for their futures and paved the way for their continued involvement with international agencies in the decade that followed.

Students and young people worked to ensure people knew where, when and how to register and, subsequently, to vote. Militia violence caused delays in ballot registration that forced a three-week postponement of the ballot until the end of August, necessary to enrol the 60,000 IDPs who were required to register in their home villages. The students were threatened and the RENETIL office had to be closed due to threats of violence (de Araujo 2000). Some students were killed for their efforts (ETAN 1999). Women's organisations played a crucial role in the campaign in the months leading up to the ballot (de Araujo 2000). Voter registration of over 450,000, almost all the adult population, was achieved in spite of the threats and violence.

The head of the UNAMET mission, Ian Martin, recognised that UNAMET's objective of peaceful implementation of the consultation process was not going to be achieved, but a further postponement would make it unlikely that the ballot would proceed at all (Martin 2000). Due to the determination that the UN sponsored ballot should go ahead, the ballot was held on 30 August 1999. On polling day 98.5 percent of registered voters turned out, in spite of the continuing threats of violence. This was a show of grim determination by the Timorese, in which a massive 78.5 percent voted *against* autonomy within Indonesia and for independence (Martin 2000). The international presence in East Timor had given people confidence to turn out even though they nevertheless anticipated retribution.

It came. The post-ballot rampage by the militia and Indonesian security forces resulted in almost 1,500 people losing their lives across the country. In one of the most horrific events of a terrible year, on the morning 6 September 1999, at 9 am, three priests and 115 refugees sheltering in the church in Suai were gunned down.[18] In a well-planned military operation 250,000 East Timorese, a third of the population, were herded by the military at gunpoint onto trucks and transported across the border to West Timor (CAVR 2005), reputedly to show the world that many Timorese were opposed to independence and frightened to stay there.[19]

The violence extended to the destruction of most of the infrastructure that the Indonesian government had built, along with houses of pro-independence supporters. Seventy percent of buildings were destroyed, including thousands of houses, schools, health clinics and administration buildings across the country. The Portuguese buildings such as the Government Palace in Dili were left unharmed. Dili was abandoned. A quarter of the population had been forcibly removed to West Timor and the remaining population fled to the mountains.

Most UN personnel and other expatriate staff had been evacuated to Darwin. Several weeks later, on 20 September 1999, INTERFET peacekeepers arrived in Dili. International agencies arrived to find near total destruction of its public records and wholesale destruction of infrastructure by the pro-Indonesian militia rampage. More than 8,000 largely Indonesian civil servants, including most of the teachers, had fled the country (Freitas 2005). The international community appeared to be unprepared for this outcome, although it has been suggested that Australia was deliberately turning a blind eye to what their intelligence agencies were telling them (Fernandes 2008).[20]

---

18   Interview, Vicente, Suai, 7 August 2006.

19   I heard a number of such accounts including from Caritas East Timor staff and many others in more recent years.

20   The Australian Government continued to insist that 'rogue elements' of the Indonesian military (TNI) were behind the violence. The final report of the Commission for Truth and Friendship Indonesia – Timor-Leste which was set up to investigate the events of 1999, has confirmed that the TNI was behind the atrocities and had backed the Timorese militia groups in the killing, rape and destruction that took place in 1999.

In October 1999 the UN established a civil administration, the United Nations Transitional Administration in East Timor (UNTAET), which would, in its first act of UN sovereignty, administer the country until independence (Chopra 2002). The emergency response planning process and coordination began in Darwin, with Dili abandoned and houses burning, and a huge emergency relief effort was mounted, which involved hundreds of foreign aid agencies. UNTAET assumed all executive and legislative authority for the transitional state, operating with a $700m budget from UN member states until formal independence was granted (Smillie and Minear 2004).

The history of struggle is a critical factor in the way the Timorese people responded to the post-conflict interventions that followed. The brutality, forced removals, hardship and misery that most people had experienced during the occupation period would be replaced by a new era, in an independent Timor-Leste, that would work in the interests of the population. Most Timorese had high expectations that their lives would be rapidly improved.

Chapter Two

A NEW INVASION: HUMANITARIAN AID AND THE GROWTH OF CIVIL SOCIETY

An international response that follows a national calamity, whether due to violent conflict or natural disaster, can have a lasting impact on the development trajectory of the afflicted country. After having virtually no outsiders present in the twenty-four years since the Indonesian invasion, East Timor experienced the arrival of a large United Nations (UN) peacekeeping operation and forty-nine humanitarian NGOs in a matter of months. This had a significant impact on the social, economic and political environment.

This chapter explores the early international development intervention in East Timor and the roles of activists from the clandestine youth and student movements who turned their focus to contribute to the internationally funded development activities following independence. The establishment and growth of civil society organisations is analysed, highlighting the attitudes of Timorese activists to the UN administration and humanitarian aid response.

The Transition of Timorese Civil Society

Activists of the clandestine student and youth organisations immediately sought ways to engage in development activities in the new political environment. This is evidenced by the examples of two key student organisations that adopted clear strategies with regard to their role in the nation's development: the National Resistance of East Timorese Students (RENETIL), the organisation of university students studying in Indonesia, and the East Timor Student Solidarity Council (ETSSC) formed by students at UNTIM university in Dili after the fall of Suharto in 1998.

Some 2000 members of RENETIL, students during the occupation, had sworn to remain faithful to the organisation, based on the mandate to 'prepare professionals with a revolutionary conscience to continue the liberation struggle through national reconstruction'.[1] RENETIL had held a Congress after the fall of Suharto in 1998 at which members discussed what the future role of the organisation might be. The Congress redefined the aims and goals of RENETIL, recognising the importance of civil society organisations in carrying out the new mission of the organisation 'to free the people from poverty, illiteracy and disease'.[2] Members at this time formed the *Sahe Institute for Liberation*, to focus on popular education, returning to Dili in 1999 to start literacy programs and to publish a magazine to open public debate. Sahe Institute engaged in transforming activists of the resistance into activists for community development and participatory democracy. Its influence spread when in 2002 the *Dai Popular Network* was formed, bringing together over twenty local NGOs and community-based organisations using popular education in their community organising work (Durnan 2009:274–5). RENETIL members also established community radio stations in Dili and many district centres, all run by local young people. Their strategy was to work through local organisations in the areas of civic education, development, environmental sustainability and advocacy. RENETIL activists thus committed themselves to the reconstruction and development of their country. As explained by one:

> The liberation of Timor-Leste was the factor that united the people. Now the focus is on liberation of the people – how to free the people from poverty, illiteracy and disease. The constitution of RENETIL focussed on how to translate this into programs.[3]

The organisation of students studying in the university in Dili, ETSSC, also felt a commitment to ongoing work for their new country and adjusted their aspirations accordingly:

> The Student Solidarity Council was established to struggle for independence, promote dialogue between Timorese and promote non-violence, to bring people with different political orientation together in dialogue. We have a moral responsibility to the country.[4]

---

1   The Internal Statute of RENETIL, article 2º, nº3. 'A RENETIL se incumbe da preparação de profissionais elevados de consciência revolucionaria para continuar a Luta de Liberação do Povo Maubere através da Reconstrução Nacional de Timor-Leste' (http://forum-haksesuk.blogspot.com/2007/04/pd-hetan-influencia-husi-kultura.html).
2   Interview, Samala Rua, Dili, 31 June 2006.
3   Interview Samala Rua, Dili, 31July 2006.
4   Interview Gusmão Soares, Dili, 29 July 2006.

A student activist in ETSSC in the mid-1990s, Natalino Gusmão Soares became Coordinator of ETSSC after independence and coordinated the National Unity Committee for civil society engagement in promoting peace during the 2006 crisis.
He is now a community development lecturer at the National University.

From its inception, ETSSC was involved in civic education, traveling into the districts to promote democracy and human rights: 'In the village we sit and talk together with young people' explained the Coordinator.[5] He further described the organisation as having 'a dream to build the nation' with its role as a 'social and moral force' to promote peace, democracy and human rights in the country, noting that the English and computer training provided by ETSSC to youth in Dili after independence 'does not respond to the goal' of promoting dialogue and non-violence. ETSSC, like other student and youth organisations were challenged by the loss of a uniting goal. A new form of civil society was required to meet the needs of a very different kind of social and political environment.

ETSSC members created new organisations to meet the demands of the new political environment. Their women's wing had a large female student membership, and this transformed into an active women's development

5   Interview Gusmão Soares, Dili, 29 July 2006.

NGO, *Grupo Feto Foinsa'e Timor Lorosa'e* (Young Women's Group – GFFTL) to run literacy and livelihood programs for women. Another is *Kadalak Sulimutuk Institute* (*KSI*) which was formed by ETSSC in 2000 as a conflict management group but became an NGO involved in research and community participation activities, especially in the area of land conflict resolution. A number of organisations transformed from operating on a membership basis to operating as NGOs. This included changing their vision from political activism to developmental operations, which some did in order to access donor funds (Ostergaard 2005:36).

Not all clandestine youth organisations found a space for themselves in the new environment. A youth social analysis study funded by the World Bank in 2005 found that the youth organisations of the resistance 'all confessed that what made their members interested in their organisation was the vision to struggle for the liberation of the country' (Ostergaard 2005). The report shows how, after independence, many youth organisations lost their central purpose, and there was uncertainty about precisely what type of role they might play in the new environment. Some became inactive with no clear direction, some affiliated as youth wings of political parties and others became development NGOs.

Activists who participated in this research expressed their ideological commitment to development, as described by one:

> Development is to change in a meaningful and positive way and to do something for our nation … development is not just for people who sit in the government but for civil society to participate in the processes.[6]

These views parallel those of evolving participatory development discourses that have emphasised practices of social analysis, community participation, gender sensitivity, and empowerment of local people as crucial ingredients for effective development. Civil society organisations are seen as fundamental to this inclusive form of development. Development, then, in the minds of these activists, is not something done by the government for the people, rather a process through which the people as active citizens combat poverty and ensure access for poor people to basic human rights.

Understanding Civil Society

The term 'civil society' is used in different ways and it is difficult to find an agreed definition. Civil society is generally understood to be the space

---

6   Interview de Carvalho, Dili, 25 August 2006.

outside the government and market, a definition based on 'what it is not' and often referred to as the *third sector* and equated with voluntary and non-profit organisations. Organised groups that make up civil society range from registered groups such as NGOs and church organisations to informal community based organisations (CBOs) such as women's groups or youth groups. Civil society in Timor-Leste has been described as 'a wide range of organisations and traditional, relatively informal, social forms and networks which are not motivated by profit' (Hunt 2008:8), a definition which recognises traditional as well as modern forms of organisation. Civil society organisations (CSOs) can be aspirational, providing a forum for a vision of a better world, as expressed by many Timorese activists.

Civil society activity has been shown to be more than just a process of providing social services or implementing development projects. An active civil society has been shown to contribute to notions of belonging and citizenship. Research has shown people's sense of citizenship, dignity and self-respect is enhanced by their engagement in civil society actions. Indeed, participation in social movements, even when acting in opposition to the state, can contribute to a sense of citizenship (Eyben and Ladbury 2006). This was evident in East Timor where the independence movement was the driver which enabled the population to unite in an organised and sustained campaign.

The active participation of Timorese activists in local organisations is clearly linked to their sense of belonging as Timorese citizens. Activism is an important part of nation building and the importance of participation in the affairs of the nation or 'active citizenship' is critical to both democracy and development (Gaventa 2006). Citizen engagement through local associations, social movements and campaigns and formal participatory government spaces, researched and documented across more than twenty countries, found that local associations were foremost in playing 'important roles in constructing citizenship, improving practices of participation, strengthening accountability and contributing to social cohesion' (Gaventa and Barrett 2012:2407). Further, local associations were the principle type of citizen engagement that most nurtured positive outcomes in settings where democracy was fragile or weak.

Local associations or civil society organisations have been closely associated with democratic governance since the work of Alexis de Tocqueville in 19th century USA. De Tocqueville observed the importance of free human association in a society which claims to be democratic, while in 20th century Italy Robert Putnam suggested active engagement in community affairs was a pre-condition for democracy (Howell and Pearce

2001). Today, the role of CIVICUS, the global alliance of civil society organisations, aims 'to amplify the voices and opinions of ordinary people'. It recognises that, for effective and sustainable civic participation to occur, citizens must enjoy rights of free association and be able to engage all sectors of society'.[7] Democratic participation is thus widely associated with civil society action.

Non-government organisations (NGOs) are typically comprised of the better-educated, socially aware, relatively privileged 'middle' social sector (Pearce 2000:39). Globally, the 1960s and 70s idea of 'helping' organisations as charities has been largely replaced within NGOs by a human rights and advocacy approach. Indeed, the concept of the 'rights based approach to development' was formulated to shift the emphasis from 'meeting basic needs' to that of promoting human rights through advocacy, citizens' participation and engagement with government structures. The rights-based approach emphasises the accountability role of civil society organisations to challenge governments and to advocate for human rights, defined in national laws or signed UN conventions.

NGOs and other local civil society organisations (CSOs) are sought after by international agencies for roles in service delivery. Howell and Pearce describe a 'mainstream perspective' in which the most immediate roles for civil society are service delivery and holding the government accountable (Howell and Pearce 2001:30–1). In this view the social solidarity role of civil society organisations is an integral component of capitalist development, whereby donor concerns about corruption and misuse of aid can be tempered by a strong civil society. Government aid and development agencies have tended to support this role as part of a process of modernisation and to assist the transition from traditional forms of production (Howell and Pearce 2001:2). The World Bank has evolved its relationships from purely economic actors to include civil society, because: 'Partnerships and participation in state activities by external stakeholders – business and civil society – can build credibility and consensus and supplement low-state capability', according to its 1997 World Development Report.

An 'alternative' view of civil society places civil society in a role of challenging dominant policies and development strategies and putting forward alternative approaches (Howell and Pearce 2001:36–7). It is this alternate view that shaped the development of civil society in Timor-Leste during the Indonesian occupation. International donors have, on the other

---

7   CIVICUS website https://www.civicus.org/en/about-us. Accessed 8 August 2012.

hand, predominantly supported the mainstream approach in the emergency, rehabilitation and development phases of international assistance. With the proliferation of new NGOs that were set up in response to the emergency and relief operations in 1999–2002 in Timor-Leste, inevitably some new NGOs with less altruistic motives grew, for example to obtain funding to generate self-employment opportunities in rural areas.

The rapid growth of CSOs is typical of international post-conflict interventions where civil society grows to meet the demands of international aid. For example, in independent Mozambique NGOs started to form only after the arrival there of international aid programs in the late 1980s. During FRELIMO's[8] Marxist-Leninist period of rule in the mid-1980s, civil society was made up of just three mass organisations for women, youth and workers, and the country was largely shunned by international aid and development agencies. Following the Mozambique government's adoption of a free-market economy, aid started to flow again and hundreds of Mozambican NGOs formed to meet the needs of international organisations as local implementing partners.

It has been suggested that co-option of civil society resulting from market ideology and globalisation can reinforce a two tier society and erode democratic ideals (Figueira-McDonough 2001:162–4). For example the 'projectisation' of the development processes in the Guatemalan Peace Process caused civil society leaders to lose touch with the grassroots base of poor and marginalised communities. The rapid emergence of civil society in response to donor requirements led to strengthened organisational hier-archies and accountability to donors but weakened accountability to its grass-roots base (Howell and Pearce 2001:157–172).

Civil society should be supported to encourage democratic ideals and social inclusion, but when humanitarian and aid agencies view local organisations just as service delivery partners, they may overlook activists' own purposes for establishing organisations. This, rather than donor-driven activities, is the source of their credibility in the community.

UNTAET Administration and the Humanitarian Response

In the early emergency and rehabilitation phase, many aid workers arrived in Dili with vast experience of emergency work in Rwanda, Bosnia and other

---

8   Mozambican Liberation Front (*Frente de Libertação de Moçambique* – FRELIMO)

post-conflict settings, but had no knowledge or understanding of Timor-Leste. Most international workers were unaware of the reality that the Timorese had been living in prior to the events of 1999, or of the twenty-four years of intimidation, fear and trauma under Indonesian military occupation. In 1999, local NGOs and civil society groups had been the target of direct and severe attacks against individuals and properties. As international agencies moved into East Timor, many NGO staff had not yet returned to Dili and others were trying to rescue what was left of their offices and materials (Brunnstrom 2003:312). It was 'several months before relief operations began benefiting from much-needed local knowledge and expertise and even when NGO staff were ready to resume work, it was common to see experienced and talented Timorese employed as drivers, interpreters and security guards' (Brunnstrom 2003:313).

The Special Representative of the Secretary-General, United Nations for Timor-Leste, Sergio Vieira de Mello, described the challenges facing the international response in 1999:

> About half of the population is illiterate. Some teachers continue to teach but receive no salaries. Most of the technicians who ran public utilities, those who ensured there was electricity and running water, have left. There are no national police, no judges either. Law and order rely largely on the goodwill of inhabitants. There is no civil registration, no banking system, no official currency, no revenue system, not even an official language. We are starting from scratch. (Sergio Vieira de Mello speech at the Donors Meeting for East Timor, Tokyo, 19 Dec 1999.)

This statement was to have repercussions as a huge humanitarian relief and reconstruction effort was implemented based on the idea of 'starting from scratch'.

Some forty-nine international NGOs (INGOs), many that had no previous connection with the country, arrived in the country in the last three months of 1999, and the number had grown to more than 250 within two years. Most of which came without funds but were looking to obtain grants from donor agencies (Smillie and Minear 2004:69). These international organisations needed to establish partnerships with local organisations and thus encouraged new local NGOs to form as partners. During the Indonesian period the civil society sector included youth organisations, women's organisations, co-operatives, church organisations, community groups and associations that had been highly active mostly in support of the independence struggle. But INGOs were looking for sets of administrative skills amongst local NGOs, to assist in the delivery of programs, that were largely unobtainable. Timorese had little experience of the forms or mechanisms of accountability required by INGOs as knowledge of applied community development skills and project management procedures was often weak (Patrick 2001:60). During the period of Indonesian military rule, information was closely guarded within families and was never written down because of the risks involved. Civil society organisations which supported the clandestine movement flourished in Timor prior to 1999, but the kind of organisations that donors wanted to work with, with experience in project management and donor funding, simply did not exist (Patrick 2001).

In Timor-Leste, from just fourteen local NGOs that had begun to undertake human rights and advocacy work when the umbrella organisation FONGTIL (NGO Forum) was established in 1998, there were some 200 local NGOs registered by the end of 2001 (Hunt 2008:311). Hunt's study of six of the more mature Timorese NGOs through the period of transition showed that many Timorese organisations did work hard to transform themselves to meet the changing external environment (Hunt 2008).

Timorese NGO representatives were disappointed by the poor knowledge of and lack of interest in local history, culture and tradition on the part of international development personnel (Brunnstrom 2003). Brunnstrom contends this failure stems from a Eurocentric orientation on the part of the international community and the assumption, 'common among international organisations: namely that of assuming that the systems and institutions that function best are those created in the image of those dominant in Western countries' (Brunnstrom 2003:314). A gulf between the Timorese and Western aid workers resulted from the top down Western attitude to development which makes 'its presence an invasion and which prevents Timorese organisations from shaping the future of their country' (Brunnstrom 2003:319).

This gulf existed both in relation to INGOs and the UN administration. The UN processes sidelined the National Council of Timorese Resistance (CNRT),[9] the political organisation under which different political parties had united in the lead up to the independence ballot, because it was considered a political organisation even though it was the de-facto voice of

---

9   The *Conselho Nacionale de Resistencia Timorense* (CNRT) included FRETILIN, UDT and some smaller parties.

the people. CNRT was left without a building to establish itself in Dili, instead having to locate themselves in Aileu District, ninety minutes away, without transport or any other support (Hunt, Bano et al. 2001). As UNTAET believed it was important to get programs operational as quickly as possible, it initiated the processes of forming structures of government but was slow to invite Timorese to work alongside it (Freitas 2005). CNRT policies and expertise were ignored.

Prior to 2000, the Timorese leadership had devised a clear and detailed trajectory for the transition to self-government and nation-building through the Magna Carta (Morison 2009:183).[10] For example CNRT had established policies with regard to the future education system, but the recruitment of teachers to replace the Indonesian teachers was directed in English to UNTAET education officers, and not to the CNRT Education Committee (Nicolai 2004:116). Further, the recruitment of the military and police forces was carried out according to entirely pragmatic considerations, such as prior experience in the force, even though the members of these two forces were at the heart of political confrontation during the Indonesian occupation just months previously. The consequences of this were to be evident in the outbreak of rivalries between the police and military which occurred during the crisis of 2006 (Rees 2003; Rosser 2008). Similarly, Timorese views on health were overridden by the World Bank's domination of fiscal policy, resulting in the numbers of health workers being set at half of that during the Indonesian period, due to budget restrictions (van Schoor 2005). New agricultural policies reflected the free market views of the World Bank rather than those of Timorese leaders, who desired farmers to be supported to resume farming following the material losses and destruction of 1999 (Anderson 2006).

Overall, the state building responsibilities taken on by international institutions resulted in sometimes hasty, unilateral decision-making about national structures and systems of administration which failed to integrate Timorese nationals into political and administrative leadership functions (Bugnion C et al. 2000; Hunt, Bano et al. 2001; Hurford and Wahlstom 2001). Some Timorese activists viewed this as a new form of colonialism, marked by patronising values about the helplessness of the populace and imposition of pre-packaged and inappropriate solutions

---

10   The CNRT held a meeting in the lead up to independence which outlined the principles concerning freedoms, rights, duties and guarantees for the people of East Timor, based on the *Magna Carta*, on which an independent state of Timor-Leste would be based. This was adopted at the East Timorese National Convention in the Diaspora in Peniche, Portugal on 25 April 1998.

(Patrick 2001:57). One report identifies the lack of Timorese participation in the humanitarian response as one of the major flaws in an otherwise very successful operation:

> One recurring issue within both the documentation and amongst interviewees was the lack of participation of East Timorese people in the early overall humanitarian aid response – either as individuals, or within NGOs, communities, churches, the CNRT and other groupings (Hurford and Wahlstom 2001:23).

The top down decision making of the UN mission was criticised early on by Timorese leader Xanana Gusmão, who accused UNTAET staff of cultivating neo-colonialist attitudes on the basis of UNTAET's unfettered political power and the economic inequality between Timorese and UNTAET staff (Philpott 2006). At a conference in Melbourne in 2005, Mari Alkatiri, Timor-Leste's first Prime Minister, described the UN mission as being established with 'imperial powers' more accountable to New York than to the Timorese people (Alkatiri 2005).

Humanitarian operations (incorporating emergency relief, reconstruction and rehabilitation) are typically managed in separate sections of aid and development organisations rather than by the staff involved in in-country partnerships. The rise of global NGO networks has led to a greater focus on global organisational plans, with increasing 'corporate' demands on staff in the field to comply with organisation goals for programming and finance. Caritas Australia was one of the few INGOs supporting local Timorese initiatives during the Indonesian occupation. It had strong in-country relationships with its partner Caritas Dili (Wigglesworth 2006). At the start of the emergency, Caritas Australia sought leadership of the emergency program within the Caritas network. With no previous emergency experience, Caritas Australia brought in emergency specialists whose different modes of operation eventually led to a breakdown with the local partner organisation. As an evaluation concluded:

> The emergency operation role of Caritas Australia in conducting the food aid operations as a contractor to the World Food Program seriously strained the partnership with Caritas Dili.[11] Caritas Australia's work as an INGO responding to the peoples' needs overshadowed its role as a Caritas partner (Hunt 2002).

---

11   With the formation of the diocese of Baucau in 1998 another Caritas Baucau was formed and Caritas East Timor became Caritas Dili.

Dili became a meeting place of old friends who had worked together in emergencies in Rwanda, Kosovo or Afghanistan, with a dual economy in which shops and restaurants catered for the international community at prices that Timorese could not afford, leaving the Timorese impoverished in a sea of plenty (Wigglesworth 2006:174). The international relief program implemented in East Timor in 1999–2000 was hailed inter-nationally as a tremendous success, but according to some this flurry of assistance following twenty-four years of inaction in East Timor 'exemplified many of the worst failing of donor agencies and governments' (Smillie and Minear 2004:51). This highlighted the dominant role of international organisations which found it easier 'to set up from this ground zero position with little local politics to worry about' (Smillie and Minear 2004:78).

Pre-existing skills, knowledge of local communities, specific community needs and local decision making processes and structures were thus largely ignored. Indeed, a review of the humanitarian response in May 2000 noted there was no framework agreement established between UN agencies or INGOs working with local organisations to ensure East Timorese participation (Bugnion C et al. 2000). The local NGOs' lack of technical skills was itself a product of the isolation and repression. The marginalisation of local NGOs that occurred in the emergency and initial rehabilitation phases of the international assistance program in East Timor had a negative impact on recovery and failed to contribute to the development of a vital civil society (Patrick 2001:63).

Capacity Building and Donor Driven Projects

The Timorese diaspora returned after the departure of the Indonesian administration and were seen by the international community as holding greater skills than local populations who 'lacked capacity' for the national administration (Hughes 2011:1504).

Where changes have taken place in the context in which people operate, such as in Timor-Leste, there will be a need for capacity development to adjust to a changing external environment (James 2001:6). Capacity dev-elopment,[12] or capacity building, refers to strengthening the capacities of

---

12   Capacity development, more commonly known in Australia as capacity building, refers
      to funded activities aimed at strengthening the work of the CSO rather than supporting
      program activities. A Timorese activist criticised the term 'capacity building' as
      implying starting from zero, arguing in favour of the term 'capacity development'.

individuals or organisations to undertake defined tasks and activities: a natural part of the process of change.

Following the emergency and rehabilitation periods, when funding levels fell and many post-1999 NGOs closed down, a number of INGOs turned their attention to enhancing capacity development in local NGOs (Hunt 2008). The need for strengthening local NGOs is undisputed, although the focus of this strengthening can be a cause of disagreement between local and international actors. In a 2006 consultation, Timorese NGO staff most commonly reported receiving training in project proposal writing, reporting and financial accountability and other project implementation requirements (Wigglesworth and Soares 2006). They claimed to have had little opportunity for institutional strengthening such as participative community engagement processes, organisational development (strategic planning, staff job roles and work plans, forming and managing a Board). Except for a few notable exceptions, INGOs have favoured 'capacity development' reflecting project accountability to donors.[13]

That 'capacity building' as devised by donors rather than in response to local demand may not strengthen civil society organisations as anticipated is demonstrated by two multi-year, multi-million dollar 'civil society strengthening projects' established in Timor-Leste soon after independence. The UNDP project 'Strengthening capacity of CSOs in local and national development processes for the achievement of millennium development goals (MDGs) in Timor-Leste 2003–6', aimed to 'enhance the capacity of CSOs in monitoring and advocacy with regard to national development goals, MDGs and NDP'.[14] The evaluators found that the project had underachieved due to its unrealistic goals, suggesting that this could have been avoided by a more participatory approach to project design and recognition that CSOs have, and want, support for their own agendas (Methven 2006). The agenda of achieving the MDGs met the needs of the UNDP and not the civil society organisations (CSOs) in the program.

Another civil society capacity-strengthening project, the Catholic Relief Services (CRS) Engaging Civil Society Project, used a two-tier process working with national NGOs as core partners to support 'satellite' CSOs in a 'cascade' model. It aimed to increase capacities of core and satellite groups through building networks and coalitions aimed at enhanced advocacy capacities amongst CSOs (Kinghorn, Pires et al. 2005). The evaluation found

---

13   Interview, Director of FONGTIL, Dili 4 October 2006.
14   NDP-National Development Plan. In the first years the project had a broader aim but changed its approach mid-stream due to UNDP funding constraints.

that assumptions made in the design were incorrect and the 'capabilities, priorities and commitments of the partners were often a mismatch for the expectations of the project'. Partner organisations were at a formative stage of development, most needing to develop mission and vision statements and to put in place basic operational structures. Neither networking nor advocacy (the focus of the project) were CSO priorities. As well, the lack of decentralisation of government structures meant that district government representatives lacked decision-making authority. Therefore there was no responsible local authority as a focus for local CSOs advocacy (Kinghorn, Pires et al. 2005). These two 'civil society strengthening' projects are examples of donor designed projects based on their own organisational priorities rather than those of the local organisations they aim to support. Ambitious projects with large budgets are often favoured by international agencies to provide long-term secure funding for their activities, sometimes developed with minimal consultation with local stakeholders. These projects typically have inflexible objectives and activities with onerous reporting that often result in the use of expatriate managers rather than building management skills of local staff.

Project managers are tasked to fulfil project objectives, activities and budgets for their organisations. Institutional demands for 'accountability' have become increasingly strident over the last decade, encouraging greater focus on the internal rather than external aspects of accountability. Long timeframes for project design and funding approval and inadequate local participation can result in a project not responding to community preferences. Rather than be responsible for implementing development best practice, project managers may be unwilling or unable to question the adequacy of the design. Both local and international staff may be judged 'accountable' by implementing the existing project design, rather than making modifications to better reflect the actual situation on the ground.

Partnerships between international donors and their local counterparts reflect a power imbalance where the donor holds all the power, even though international NGOs may have altruistic motives outlined in their vision and mission statements. Research into NGO aid effectiveness with Australian NGOs found that a value base is critical to playing an effective development role (Chapman and Kelly 2007). The NGO's compliance with its organisational values enabled it to achieve effective program outcomes. Importantly, long term relationships in developing countries which allowed partners to work together in trust and mutual learning to resolve issues and problems were found to be the key to effective funding partnerships (Chapman and Kelly 2007).

An example of this trust and mutual learning occurred in the Irish NGO Concern in Timor-Leste. Concern's partner agency staff were invited into Concern staff meetings at which internal organisational issues were exposed to the scrutiny of their partners (as a capacity building exercise) so the partners could see and learn from the experience that all agencies have problems for which they need to seek solutions (Wigglesworth 2008:10). Such partnerships are described by Fowler as 'authentic partnerships' where dialogue and mutual understanding underpins decision making about activities including capacity development, and the donor is held accountable by the local NGO for what is said and done (Fowler 2002).

In the early years of independence the relationship between government and civil society was fragile. The role of civil society as a 'watch dog' in keeping the government accountable was viewed positively by the World Bank, which noted that NGOs provided 'useful monitoring, advocacy, education and advisory services in the areas of human rights (*Associação HAK*), justice (*JSMP* – Judicial System Monitoring Program), gender awareness (*Fokupers, Rede Feto*), the environment (*Haburas*) and international assistance (*La'o Hamutuk*) (World Bank 2005:3). As the NGO Forum (FONGTIL) started to play a strong advocacy role in relation to the Timor Sea oil, land ownership and fiscal transparency, this did not always please the government. The tension between the government and civil society mirrored that which existed in the Indonesian period, according to one activist: 'the Timorese government has the Indonesian idea of distrust of NGOs'.[15] This view was echoed by the World Bank: 'The Government is hesitant to collaborate with civil society and maintains a statist style. It has not yet succeeded in engaging constructive critics or in maintaining an effective dialogue with communities' (World Bank 2005:4).

During the resistance a common enemy existed, but now with independence the government did not appear to like the independent thinking arising from civil society organisations. This was partly because many young Timorese had defected from FRELILIN to join the new Democratic Party set up by former RENETIL leader Fernando de Araujo. Civil society organisations thus sometimes became seen as 'oppositional' rather than a potential source of people with capacity to contribute to the development processes. As described by one academic: 'The government sees civil society as the opposition and the opposition as the enemy'.[16]

---

15   Interview with Oxfam former Country Director, 27 March 2007.
16   Interview with Director of Dili Institute of Technology (DIT), Dili, 6 September 2006.

Summary

When the international aid community arrived in Timor-Leste they replaced and displaced Timorese decision making. The Timorese disappointment with the perceived take-over by Western development agencies compromised the relationships between the international community and Timorese. Foreign agencies did not recognise that the Timorese had been planning for independence and had clear ideas of what kind of arrangements they wanted to put in place.

Large scale international emergency and rehabilitation programs generate a rapid growth of local civil society organisations to meet service delivery requirements. When NGOs implement donor-funded programs there is often an unequal relationship between the international donor agencies and local organisations. This can limit options for local agencies and constrain altruistic NGO values and locally defined development.

As an integral part of nation building, civil society should assist in citizens having voice and taking up advocacy or promoting practical interventions in support of the rights and needs of the population. Effective partnerships require mutual learning between international and local organisations so that the knowledge that each brings to the process is respected equally in an 'authentic partnership'. Timorese activists emphasised the need for Timorese to define and develop programs that build on knowledge of both traditional customs and progressive understandings of individual and democratic rights. But while the beliefs, customs and practices of the majority of the Timorese people remained a strong force in Timor-Leste, political leaders from the diaspora were removed from the culture, and the international community understood little of it, with consequences that are described in the next chapter.

Chapter Three

BUILDING A STATE, RE-ESTABLISHING A NATION

Timor-Leste began its nation-rebuilding at a time when development ideologies had shifted from a twentieth-century focus on economic interventions to recognition of the importance of social issues in development, particularly issues of democracy, participation and good governance. Development theory moved away from technical strategies towards greater emphasis on people-led development and building a sense of citizenship.

When the Democratic Republic of Timor-Leste (RDTL) officially took over the reins of government from UNTAET in 2002, many of the structures and processes of governance had already been set in place by the UN. The first RDTL government nevertheless had a huge task to establish 'Pillars of the State' for a liberal democratic government (the Parliament, the Presidency and the Judiciary) and the national administration. This chapter shows how the UN and the World Bank had a primary role in policy making in East Timor after the departure of the Indonesian administration regarding both the national economy and governance processes.

International Development Institutions

In 1999 Sergio de Mello, UN Transitional Administrator for East Timor, reported at the Donors' Meeting in that year that institutions in East Timor had to 'start from scratch'. The Joint Assessment Mission (JAM) established by the World Bank had developed a blueprint policy for the nation based on this position. The JAM consultants witnessed the devastation of infra-structure and the dearth of people and came to the hasty conclusion that development, including local governance structures, would need to be wholly developed (Patrick 2001:57). At the Donors' Meeting, a Consolidated Fund for East Timor (CFET) was created to fund the administration of

East Timor by the United Nations from 1999 through multilateral and bi-lateral[1] aid contributions.

Beyond the UNTAET period a Trust Fund for East Timor (TFET) was set up under the management of the World Bank and the Asian Development Bank (ADB)[2] to mobilise international bi-lateral and multi-lateral donor development contributions for reconstruction and development activities in health, education, agriculture, transport, power, and other key sectors (World Bank and ADB 2005; Rosser 2007). This gave these two institutions considerable leverage in the country.

Their influence, however, was not entirely welcome by the new government. The World Bank and other agencies encouraged the new government of Timor-Leste to borrow money in order to invest in coffee, vanilla or palm oil production for export (Moxham 2004). The first Prime Minister, Mari Alkatiri, who lived in Mozambique during the occupation, was totally opposed to financing development through foreign assistance loans because RDTL did not want to become indebted and wished to avoid the 'debt trap' (Molnar 2010:117). The Timorese government sought to limit the financial influence of the World Bank and was unwilling to make loan arrangements that would provide the Bank with leverage over economic policy.

While key leaders of the first Timorese government were in Mozambique, the external headquarters of FRETILIN's Central Committee, during the Indonesian occupation (Scott 2005), they experienced the powerful influences of the international finance institutions (IFIs). Mozambique, which like Timor-Leste became independent in 1975 as a result of the change of government in Portugal, was forced to adopt economic restructuring in exchange for development finance. Some members of FRELIMO had adopted a Marxist-Leninist ideology during its independence struggle against Portuguese colonialism. When FRELIMO came into power at independence, the country was shunned by Western nations. Rhodesia,

---

1   Bi-lateral aid is country to country aid by national government agencies. Multi-lateral aid includes donors such as UN agencies (UNDP, UNICEF, WHO, FAO etc.) and international financial institutions (World Bank, IMF, Asian Development Bank etc). The donor Organisation for Economic Cooperation and Development (OECD) countries support market-based development programs both through their own bi-lateral programs and through their contribution to the multilateral agencies.

2   TFET is a multi-donor trust fund that has supported reconstruction and development activities in Timor-Leste since 2000. The Government of Timor-Leste in coordination with the World Bank, the ADB, TFET donors, and other stakeholders, established TFET program priorities. All activities are implemented by Government agencies with support from stakeholders.

and later South Africa, created and backed a militia army, RENAMO,[3] to destabilise the fledgling government, destroy national infrastructure and terrorise the population, (Hanlon 1986:140). A decade and a half of war brought Mozambique to economic collapse. The FRELIMO government was forced to negotiate with the IMF and World Bank and accepted an IMF financial package in 1987 in return for adopting free market and social democratic policies. Mozambique became one of the world's highly aid dependent and indebted countries, a status that Timor-Leste's political leaders were, upon assuming power, anxious to avoid.

The two key IFIs, the International Bank for Reconstruction and Development (known as the World Bank) and the International Monetary Fund (IMF) were formed at a conference in Bretton Woods in 1944 to plan and finance the rebuilding of Europe after the Second World War. This was the end of the colonial era, heralding a new approach to the first world–third world relationships. Development aid was established as a means of funding infrastructural support in newly independent countries. In this era, 'development' was perceived as a linear process of stages of development from pre-capitalist to fully fledged capitalist economies through transfer of Western technology, knowledge and capital. The ideas were encapsulated in the 'Stages of economic growth' theory of the 1960s, which held that a transfer of capital and skills to underdeveloped countries would improve people's livelihoods and standards of living as a by-product and consequence of 'modernisation' (Remenyi 2004:25). This view was challenged by Latin American economists who believed that developed countries had advanced economically through the extraction of cheap resources from their colonies, elaborated in their 'Dependency Theory' (McKay 2004:54). Underdevelopment was a process, not simply a condition, they claimed, and the wealth of the 'first world' or 'developed' countries was the result of the exploitation of 'third world' or 'developing' countries' natural resources via ever-worsening terms of trade. Growing inequalities between the first and third worlds, it was argued, prevented developing countries from achieving the levels of development seen in the West. Both theories established national economic growth as the key mechanism for development. The debate between capitalist modernisation theorists and socialist dependency theorists faded with the collapse of the communist bloc (viewed as the 'second world') and the subsequent unchallenged dominance of the free market (Schuurman 1993).

---

3   Mozambican National Resistance or *Resistência Nacional Moçambicana*.

Since the 1980s the World Bank and IMF have been at the centre of major global economic policy-making based on free market strategies which became a policy requirement for developing countries to receive ODA[4] grants and loans (Stiglitz 2002:11). This international policy agreement was promoted by conservative governments in the UK and USA and implemented by these two Washington-based 'Bretton Woods' institutions in what is referred to as the 'Washington consensus'. Providing finance through loans to poor countries, the World Bank and IMF demanded smaller governments and the promotion of the private sector and free market as the main vehicles for development. Government subsidies and services were kept to a minimum: government policies should reduce the size of the public service; remove minimum prices and subsidies; privatise services; deregulate the economy to encourage foreign investment; and promote agricultural production for export. These neo-liberal policies bear a number of similarities to 'modernisation' discourses, as deregulated economies promoted free-market access to natural resources. According to McKay: 'some features have been redefined and reworked but the basic points about unequal power and the exploitation of the poor countries remain' (McKay 2004).

Globally, more funds have been transferred in debt repayments from poor countries to rich than is received by the poor in the form of aid. Some economists argue that open market policies did not contribute to reducing poverty in less developed countries (Mosley, Harrigan et al. 1995; Killick 1998; White 2001). The 1980s became known as the 'lost decade' in development, where reforms failed to produce sustained growth, incomes fell, and the gap between rich and poor widened, particularly in Latin America (Jaquette and Staudt 2007). Countries with low levels of human resource development and poor infrastructure were at a disadvantage when competing in an open market. The high-growth 'Asian Tigers' of Singapore, South Korea, Hong Kong and Taiwan, claimed as proof of success of the development model, all invested heavily in human resources (education and health) and public infrastructure for many years before they opened their doors to the free market (Mackay 2005). In contrast, the least developed countries had to weather exposure to the free market at a time when they lacked the human capital to engage in the economic activities required for

---

4   'Official Development Assistance' (ODA) is defined by the OECD as being flows from official sources for the 'promotion of economic development and welfare of developing countries as its main objective', and as 'concessional in character with a grant element of at least 25%'. Thus concessional loans are defined as ODA while non-government organisations' grants are not.

market-driven development. This has led to an argument to invest more in human capital in the form of education and health in order to sustain growth and stem inequality (Seligson 2003:468). In the poorest countries the gap between the rich and poor has widened as a growing middle class engage in a globalised market, while the conditions of the poor have hardly changed.

In Timor-Leste, the international financial institutions had considerable influence on the direction of the new economy. World Bank approved TFET funds for proposals based on the private sector and market as vehicles for economic development. The World Bank discouraged the maintenance of a national agricultural subsidy system (as implemented during the Indonesian period), by which agricultural services provided seeds, access to tractors for ploughing for a small fee, a rice marketing system that guaranteed sales of surplus production, and subsidised seeds and fertilisers. Proposals by the Timorese leadership for agricultural support in compensation for the loss of animals and agricultural equipment taken or destroyed in 1999 were denied (Anderson 2006). According to Anderson, their requests for the use of aid money to rehabilitate rice fields, build grain silos and public abattoirs were in conflict with the free-market policies of the trustees. During the Indonesian occupation large areas of land were cultivated for rice by the Indonesian transmigrant population brought in by the Indonesian administration. The transmigrants left, the tractors were taken and the irrigation systems were destroyed by the departing Indonesians. Timorese farmers were left to cultivate using traditional hand tools, dramatically reducing the area they could cultivate. Market opportunities also shrank as the numbers of salaried public servants was halved, reducing the circulation of cash in the districts in the early years of independence.

As most Timorese agricultural produce was for family consumption[5] it fell outside the agricultural policy focus of the World Bank, which promoted production for the market. The main marketed food crop in Timor-Leste is rice, yet the World Bank discouraged Timor-Leste from rice production, arguing that rice can be produced more cheaply and imported from countries such as Indonesia and Thailand.[6] The risks of this strategy became evident when the 2008 global economic crisis caused food prices to escalate around

---

5   Subsistence farmers derive their principle food requirements from their farms. However they may market produce to variable degrees, depending on both the harvest and cash needs, for example to buy cooking oil, soap, clothes and to pay school fees. In a year of poor harvest a surplus may not exist.

6   Interview with World Bank Country Representative, Dili, 12 September 2005.

the world and much of the population of Dili was in distress due to the price of rice and forced to reduce food intake.

Measuring Development

In a significant move away from the World Bank's economic indicators of Gross Domestic Product (GDP) to measure development, a Human Development Index (HDI) established a human rights focus for development status and ranking of nations. Economist Amartya Sen was instrumental in creating the HDIs in 1990 for the United Nations Development Program (UNDP), which annually publishes HDIs for all countries, incorporating national economic and non-economic indicators such as health, education, longevity and gender differentials as a measure of development.

Human centred development, as articulated by Amartya Sen, defines 'development' broadly. Sen stated 'freedom is both the means and the end of development', arguing that 'unfreedoms' arise from structures and realities that 'limit people's reason to value their lives' (Sen 1999). Sen blamed neo-liberal strategies for generating inequalities which lead to social 'unfreedoms' which must be overcome by focussing on human capabilities and the enhancement of human potential. He did not reject market-driven development, considering the market an essential component of freedom, but argued safeguards are required so that the state can protect and support vulnerable individuals. Taking up this approach with respect to opportunities and choices for women, Martha Nussbaum suggested that the cultural assumptions of 'what women do' should be put aside to focus on 'what people are actually capable of doing' in support of empowerment and human dignity (Nussbaum 2000).

Concern about why world poverty was continuing in spite of some forty years of development assistance led to a new approach, a commitment by world leaders to free men, women and children from dehumanising poverty and share the benefits of globalisation more fairly. Just before Timor-Leste's independence, in the year 2000, the largest gathering of world leaders in history took place at the Millennium Summit at the UN in New York City. At this meeting eight key Millennium Development Goals (MDGs) were established to be achieved by the year 2015. These included halving the incidence of extreme poverty, achieving universal primary education, promoting gender equality, reducing child mortality, improving maternal health, combatting endemic diseases and strengthening environmental sustainability. Achievements are monitored and published against targets for each country in the UNDP Human Development Report. Since the MDGs became a measure of development progress, former IFI policies, such as user fees on primary education and health clinic attendance, were revised. This 'post-Washington' approach acknowledges the existence of market imperfections and embraces the idea that strong social and institutional structures are crucial to growth and development. A strategy of 'pro-poor growth' is now promoted by major development agencies, with the key policy message:

> Promoting pro-poor growth – enabling a pace and pattern of growth that enhances the ability of poor women and men to participate in, contribute to and benefit from growth – will be critical in achieving a sustainable trajectory out of poverty and meeting the Millennium Development Goals (OECD 2006).

These policy shifts also generated a view that social capital, in the form of social networks and civil institutions, are as important as other forms of capital to achieve these ends. Further, these social structures need to be supported by pluralistic forms of governance and decision making to develop social consensus over key reforms (Edwards 2001). This resulted in agencies such as the World Bank increasingly engaging with civil society in developing countries.

As well, the lack of national ownership of previous economic strategies imposed by the IFIs was seen as an impediment to progress, so donors started to seek national governments' participation and commitment to the national development programs that they supported. In 2005, a meeting on aid effectiveness committed international donors to joint planning by donors and recipients through the Paris Declaration, embracing the principles of ownership, harmonisation, alignment, results and mutual accountability in aid delivery (AusAID 2008). For this to be achieved, it is essential that national governments are active participants in the formulation of their national development plans. National government ownership of policies and development programs as well as peoples' participation in development initiatives had thus become part of mainstream policy.

Democracy and Governance Programs

Democratisation is recognised as a means by which people can participate in the process by which they are governed, and keep corrupt or dictatorial regimes out of government. UN peace keeping programs around the world have culminated in an electoral process being introduced into the 'host' country (Kumar 1998). In many cases, however, this process may be imposed on communities with little preparation or knowledge of Western style democracy, thus 'democracy' may be experienced by them as little more than an electoral process accompanied by election campaigns, adversarial politics and increased individualism.

For democracy to be a process that enables people to participate in issues that affect them, two conditions must be met. Firstly, citizen participation must be strengthened so that poor people are given a voice. This requires new forms of inclusion, consultation and mobilisation in order that those most socially disadvantaged are able to be heard by institutions and policies. Secondly, it is also necessary to strengthen the accountability and responsiveness of national institutions and policies (Gaventa 2004).

There are three spheres of government in Timor-Leste: national, local (District and Sub-District administrations) and village or *Suco*. The *Suco* level has historically been led by a *Suco* Chief chosen according to customary power structures. Both the Portuguese and Indonesian authorities collaborated with these customary power structures to maintain local authority. Indeed the Indonesian government delegated responsibilities and powers in planning, civil registry and conflict resolution tasks to the *Suco* level (Ministry of State Administration 2003).

In the UNTAET period a 'Community Empowerment Program' (CEP) was established as an outcome of the JAM. The JAM had assumed that there were no local structures with which the authorities could collaborate and proceeded to create 'representative, community based institutions in order that the emergency phase may proceed with greater efficiency and community participation' (Patrick 2001; Gunn 2003). Existing traditional leadership structures and practices within Timor-Leste that constituted local forms of decision making were ignored. The World Bank required the CEP Councils to have equal gender participation and to be made up of literate members, thus young educated people who either had some kind of 'project experience' or had proven to be good leaders in the clandestine movement were elected to the Councils. Effectively a dual structure of local authority was set up: youth on the CEP Council referred matters to customary leaders to make decisions that were then ratified at the Council meeting. According to one study, political and ritual authority are strongly connected to age thus the lack of seniority of their members meant that most of the councils had not yet developed any real power (Ospina and Hohe 2002). The World Bank's CEP Completion Report noted that the 'failure to create a sustainable institutional base for community development is a significant shortcoming in the project' (World Bank 2005). It was found that the hurry to get the project going resulted in too little time for participatory processes to be developed to allow local views to be considered in its implementation.

The establishment of Western democratic rule within a customary society requires an understanding of interlinking worlds and power structures, if new political forms are not to clash with traditional ones (Preece and Mosweunyane 2003). For people to feel included, the democratic system needed to be relevant to their reality. For example, at independence, only 14 percent of Timorese believed that primary responsibility for law and order in the community lay with the police, in comparison with 81 percent who believed that community leaders were responsible (Asia Foundation 2002). The formal court system and police were seen as less fair, less accessible and more complex than the customary system where senior men gather together for a process of inter-familial consensus decision making. Observing the top down processes for establishing governance structures a Timorese activist noted:

> Democracy is like a fruit tree which is forced to produce fruit early – it does not taste good. It has not had time to mature. Timor has not had time to mature with democracy. We need to build people's understanding of the world, especially traditional views of democratic process. Our tradition has democracy – elders come together to discuss issues where more respected people are listened to more.[7]

The CEP also aimed to 'empower' communities to manage their own development projects, building on a new paradigm in development which challenged the orthodox views of development emanating from top down bureaucratic planning systems. This drew on the 'participatory approach' of the World Bank known as Community Driven Development methodology, funded by a global budget of $5.6 billion across 2000–2002 (Moxham 2004). As part of the CEP, individual entrepreneurship was encouraged through the provision of locally administered small loans and grants for local recovery and development activities. Over half of the CEP micro-credit loans in Timor went to kiosks[8] which resulted in an oversupply of this form of micro-enterprise (Moxham 2004). In 70 percent of cases the kiosk holder was unable to make enough money to pay back the original

---

7   Interview, Timor Aid staff, Melbourne 7 April 2007.
8   Shops normally in a small hut made of locally obtained materials.

loan, and the output of this component was subsequently categorised as unsatisfactory by the World Banks' own completion report (World Bank 2005). The CEP was subject to conventional project timeframes that did not allow the 'participatory development' model to be implemented. The failure of the World Bank to implement these principles of good practice therefore left poor Timorese individuals taking on a debt burden without adequate preparation or support to increase their income. The program was bound by institutional practices that made it impossible to achieve its objectives of effective consultation, achieving neither empowerment nor development.

The first RDTL government set out its national vision in the National Development Plan (Planning Commission 2002). This initial national plan for the new country, setting out national goals and objectives, was built on a broad consultation with the Timorese people in the lead up to independence, drawing on the views of almost 36,000 people through public consultation with communities, members of the church, civil society, national and international NGOs, the private sector and public interest groups (Planning Commission 2002:xvii). This process was highly regarded by civil society activists, as one explained:

> Development is a process for the future, and includes education – free primary school for all, economic opportunity such as access to develop their own products, and justice for grassroots people, as well as participation of men and women in political leadership … During 6 years the government did many good things – the National Development Plan was good because it resulted from grassroots people with wide consultation with civil society and women's networks.[9]

These remarks imply that if development is to be worthwhile and sustainable it must enable people to engage in the process. Sadly, as we will see, a weak engagement between national policy-making and the population continued to constrain development for many years to come.

Financing Development: Oil and Aid

An important focus of government in the first years of independence was the establishment of Timor-Leste's economic independence. The Timor Gap agreement between the Australian Government and UNTAET, taken over by RDTL in May 2002, realised an income over four to five years of

---

9   Interview, Abrantes, Dili, 30 July 2006.

$80m from the Bayu Undan oil field.[10] The RDTL's national income budget was just $67.6 million the first year, $74.6 million the second year, and $75 million the third year, almost all of it from donor aid. By 2005 oil revenues started to contribute to Timor-Leste's national income. Between 2006 and 2012, the State Budget grew by a factor of five, from $262 million to $1,280 million, of which almost all was from oil revenues.[11]

Negotiations for the Timor Sea oil and gas production in the first years had forced many of the Timorese government's resources to be absorbed in a fight with the government of Australia to claim these petroleum resources (Cleary 2007). The 1972 maritime border agreement between Indonesia and Australia gave Australia two-thirds of the sea bed, access to the Timor Sea oil and gas reserves and established Australia's recognition of Indonesian sovereignty over the territory. In order to impede any challenge by Timor-Leste over the maritime boundary, Australia withdrew from the International Tribunal for the Law of the Sea in 2002 (Brennan 2004). If international maritime law had been applied, the oil and gas of the Sunrise field would have been within Timor-Leste's maritime boundary, but Australia sought to maintain the maritime boundary agreed with Indonesia. The Timor Sea Treaty signed on independence day (20 May 2002) provided for sharing of proceeds of the Joint Petroleum Development Area (JPDA). As the Greater Sunrise field is only partially within the JPDA, Timor-Leste would gain just 18 percent of revenue. Tough negotiating by the fledgling Timorese government ultimately resulted in a new Treaty on Certain Maritime Arrangements in the Timor Sea, but this required Timor-Leste to accept a fifty year deferment of the maritime boundary line settlement in exchange for an increase in royalties from the original 18 percent to 50 percent share from the proposed development of the Greater Sunrise field (Molnar 2010:105). Activists argue that if a mid-line maritime boundary was agreed, then all the Greater Sunrise would fall within Timor-Leste's borders.

The establishment of the RDTL's Petroleum Fund in September 2005 preserved the benefits of the extraction of oil and gas from the Timor Sea by investing oil and gas royalties in US bonds to create an income stream for future generations and to avoid the 'resource curse' (Drysdale 2007). Once RDTL started to receive royalties, it could start to support itself economically through interest from the Petroleum Fund, the value of which rose rapidly.

---

10   Figures in US dollars unless otherwise indicated.
11   La'o Hamutuk submission to National Parliament Committee C (Economy, Finances and Anti-corruption) regarding the General State Budget for 2011 (http://www. laohamutuk.org)

By 2007 the oil revenue had benefited from increased production at the Bayu Undan field and the rising price of oil, providing a total of $956m to the Fund in the twelve months to June 2007, with the Fund value exceeding previous expectations (La'o Hamutuk 2008). By 2011, according to Lao Hamutuk,[12] oil and gas exports paid for 97 percent of state expenditures. The quarterly report of the Central Bank of Timor-Leste (*Banco Central de Timor-Leste* – BCTL) of June 2014 shows that its capital in the Petroleum Fund was $16.6 billion.

By 2008 the Timorese government was able to make its own decisions on how to improve health, education and agricultural services, and to develop the economy. For example, during a visit to Australia the Timorese Minister of Health, Dr Nelson Martins, announced that the government was progressing with a plan to import generic drugs from countries such as Bangladesh at a fraction of the cost of the brand name drugs. He explained that when dependent on donor funds, the Ministry of Health (MoH) had been obliged to buy from the major drug companies.[13] He anticipated that the MoH would benefit from a dramatic reduction in the drug bill allowing greater expenditure in other areas, as well as providing increased government control over its spending.

A cost effective aid program for Timor-Leste was the provision in 2006 of Cuban doctors by the Cuban Government for $250 a month, ten times less that the UN-contracted expatriate doctors that they replaced. Some 230 Cuban doctors worked in Timor-Leste, while Cuban scholarships enabled 600 Timorese to attend medical school in Cuba and then replace the Cuban health professionals, following their graduation (Leach 2008). The US and Australia were not happy with the relationship that formed between Timor-Leste and Cuba (Molnar 2010:117), but in this country where doctors had previously been limited to the district towns, the Cuban health program enabled a doctor to be based in every sub-District at significantly less cost than Western aid-funded options.

Portugal has had a major influence on the development of the Timorese state from its inception, as a major donor to Timor-Leste and through Timor-Leste's membership of the Community of Portuguese speaking countries (*Comunidade dos Paises de Lingua Portuguesa* – CPLP). The Timorese Constitution was modelled after that of Portugal, with certain adaptations from Mozambique (Molnar 2010:85). Timor-Leste's adoption of the

---

12   http://www.laohamutuk.org/
13   Seminar presentation by Dr Nelson Martins, Victoria University, 8 November 2007.

Portuguese language was financed by Portuguese Cooperation, including the development of a Portuguese language school curriculum and technical assistance in teacher training. Portuguese Cooperation describes itself as working as a European Union member state and within the national development strategy of Timor-Leste to provide assistance: 'on the one hand, the consolidation of Portuguese as an official language in a wide range of contexts and, on the other, continued support towards developing an independent and effective judiciary, as well as the provision of specialist legal support to the civil service'.[14] This relationship has enabled Timor-Leste to maintain some independence from the powerful influences of the Anglophone Western nations and their agencies, although these linkages have found little support amongst the majority of the nation's young population, an issue elaborated further in chapter six.

According to the Timorese government transparency portal, in the four years 2009–2012 Portugal provided US$36 million. This can be compared to Australia, the largest donor, providing US$123 million, mostly in the strengthening of the state in the areas of policing, public sector development, the justice sector and rural water supply. The portal shows that of international commitments to Timor-Leste of $1,771 million, 57 percent or just over $1,000 million has been disbursed, with over 80 percent spent in Dili.

Another important issue in aid contributions is boomerang aid – that component which returns to the donor country as salaries and payments for goods and services. Timor-Leste's former President, Jose Ramos Horta, has been an outspoken critic of Western aid policies, claiming on a visit to Australia in July 2009 that foreign aid was being spent on East Timor but not in East Timor. Of US$3 billion pledged to the country he stated most never made it to the people: 'they claim to have spent on training, capacity building schemes. Yes, we needed that and there has been some positive use to that, but if that money was really used for capacity building in a proper way, every Timorese would have a PhD by now'.[15]

Aiming to change the power relations of international post-conflict aid, Timor-Leste played a leading role in the formation of the g7+ group of nineteen 'fragile and conflict-affected countries'. Emilia Pires, Finance Minister of Timor-Leste in the fourth and fifth RDTL governments, had a passion for aid effectiveness that led this g7+ group to present a demand for a 'New Deal for Engagement in Fragile States' at the 4th High Level Forum on Aid

---

14   Government of Portugal (2007) *Portugal-East Timor Program 2007–2010* pp.10–11.
15   Interview on ABC Radio 'Australian foreign aid to East Timor "wasted"', Connect Asia, 29 July 2009.

Effectiveness, held in Busan, South Korea in November 2011. The groups' vision was that 'development architecture and new ways of working, better tailored to the situation and challenges of fragile contexts, are necessary to build peaceful states and societies'. A key demand was that engagement should *focus on country-led and country-owned transitions out of fragility* with support of international partners for 'one vision and one plan' (International Dialogue on Peacebuilding and Statebuilding 2011). In 2012, Finance Minister Pires was nominated Chair of the g7+ as well as being appointed by the Secretary-General of United Nations Ban Ki-moon to the 'High-level Panel of Eminent Persons on the post 2015 Development Agenda'.

Timor-Leste's leadership resulted in an international conference on the post-2015 Development Agenda, the largest meeting ever held in Dili at the Convention Centre in February 2013. It was attended by 227 participants from over forty-eight countries, on the theme: 'Development for All: Stop Conflicts, Build States and Eradicate Poverty!' The meeting produced an agreement known as 'The Dili Consensus'[16] on forms of cooperation, especially global South-South cooperation, as the key driver for change.

Summary

Harsh market economic policies of the 1980s and 90s have been modified to give recognition to the fact that development is a social as well as an economic process. This is evidenced by the importance given to meeting the MDGs, embracing concepts of democracy and promoting civil society as a check on government. Aid, however, is also used as a political tool to influence national policy decisions, promote neo-liberal economic policies and Western-style democracy, often with inadequate consultation with the people affected or understanding of pre-existing governance structures.

The international intervention from 1999 onwards presumed that Western concepts of development were those that would best meet the 'development' objectives of a new nation. Initially by-passing local leadership, the introduced structures, policies and practices did not take into account the socio-cultural conditions on which they were imposed. The government of Timor-Leste now leads an international movement which espouses a greater role for host countries in decision making about aid in peacebuilding and fragile environments. Next, the social and cultural aspects of rural life will be investigated and why this leads to differential impacts of development aid on men and women.

---

16   The Dili Consensus document is available at: www.g7plus.org/storage/Dili%20
Consensus%20English%20Final.pdf

Chapter Four

BREAKING WITH TRADITION: CUSTOM AND GENDER ISSUES

An educated mother is likely to have better nourished and more healthy children, a smaller family, be more likely to seek education for her children and contribute to the family economy in a manner that can assist the family rise out of poverty (UN 2005). Gender inequality has a deleterious effect on the health and education of girls.

Timor-Leste has enshrined gender equality in the Constitution and has signed up to international standards of human rights. The national adoption of a policy of gender equality is seen by many in the rural areas as conflicting with customary practices, marked by strongly defined gender roles and responsibilities for men and women, regarded as the essence of Timorese culture. On the other hand, there is an active women's civil society network which has been instrumental in lobbying for women's rights and active in bringing about improvements in women's status nationally.

Kinship, Customs and Marriage

Over 75 percent of the total population of Timor-Leste continue to live according to what is currently understood as 'custom' in rural communities. Customary practices dictate distinct roles for men and women: women's work is defined by the domestic sphere and men are the principle decision makers. Culture, however, is dynamic and while today's customary practices may be seen as 'traditional' they may actually be relatively recent. Niner (2011) identifies the three significant external influences on the status of women in Timorese society. These are the Portuguese colonial patriarchal elite, committed to conservative Catholicism; the violent and militarised society under Indonesian occupation, during which women's roles and responsibilities shifted radically, and the international norms and gender policies of the UN administration and international agencies since 1999. In spite of changes, the rural areas remain relatively untouched:

> When travelling out of Dili the state often seems to barely touch down within communities at all … The mode of communication remains predominantly oral; forms of social hierarchy are genealogically and patriarchally framed; and the world is understood and regulated by *adat* (customs) and *lulik* (belief in sacred objects, often fusing the human with the natural world), with Roman Catholicism layered over the top … In these communities, tribal-traditional social forms tend to regulate the world in a way that the state has yet to come even close to achieving. (Grenfell 2007:11)

The majority of the population live in rural areas in scattered hamlets (*aldeias*) or villages (*sucos*) where customary leadership and links to ancestral lands remains important aspects of family life. Historically the country was divided into a number of different kingdoms, with political authority resting with the *liurai*, or king, who presided over the land. The *liurai*'s power was balanced by the *dato* who has ritual authority from the ancestral order and values from his connection with the spiritual world (Trindade 2011). In Timorese culture, there is no separate category of 'law' but '*lisan*' or custom comprises all the 'dos' and 'don'ts' in a community, such that the ancestors act as legislators and their living representatives, the *lia nain*,[1] become the judiciary (Hohe 2003:339). These individuals are responsible for resolving conflict through mediation between families and clans and for maintaining balance between people, their land and the ancestors. As ancestral rules are not written, elders in the community must 'be in contact' or 'know the word' of the ancestors (Hohe 2003:340).

The social structure includes clans which make up a hamlet organised around the clan's *uma lulik* (sacred house). The local power system is hereditary, with a class structure which stratifies the house members, with the *liurai* and *dato* at the top, the majority as landowning commoners and at the bottom of the hierarchy a lower class of 'slaves' sometimes captured from other clans (Cristalis and Scott 2005). Kinship through blood or marital relations within a lineage or extended family is defined by the formation of an *uma lulik*: members of any *uma lulik* can trace their blood relations back to a common ancestor. The hierarchical structure places ritual authority with the highest house and other tasks, including political authority with other houses. McWilliams describes the notion of a 'house' as 'a social

---

1   The role of *lia nain* is sometimes described as a 'spokesperson' or 'judicial authority'. In either case they play a ceremonial role through carrying the wisdom of the ancestors.

construction and a ritualised focus for the articulation of social relations and exchange among sacred house members' (McWilliam 2005). While the rigid class structure has now weakened, many *aldeia* and *suco* chiefs continue to be selected from families that carry traditional authority. Customary structures are central to local decision making across Timor-Leste, with some difference in social customs by different clans.

The structure determines the social and ritual life of the people, and any wrongdoing will be dealt with to restore balance. Male elders at *aldeia* and *suco* levels are responsible for resolving conflict through mediation between families and clans. Babo-Soares describes customary practice for conflict situations as seeking to mediate between opposing factions until they reach an ultimate goal of achieving continuing harmony and peace in society (Babo-Soares 2004:22).

More than a dozen major ethno-linguistic groups in Timor-Leste are divided into two major language groups – one linked to the Austro-Malay and the other to Papuan language groups. Timorese societies are patriarchal, with men holding decision making power, but in matrilineal societies in the south western part of the country, family lineage passes through women. In spite of their diversity, Timorese societies have more in common than differences. There is considerable intermarriage between groups, particularly amongst the educated elite that have moved to the capital.

Traditional structures emphasise community well-being over individual self-interest. This stands in contrast to the individualism predominant in many 'Western' societies. Social structures and customs vary between different ethno-linguistic groups, but all sacred houses play a pivotal role in establishing alliances between houses. Marriage alliances extend the family into the future through offspring and generate a peaceful bond (Trindade and Bryant 2007:20). A match, arranged by the *lia nain* of the two houses, represents a contract between the two clans in which fertility is seen to be handed over (Cristalis and Scott 2005). The marriage partners themselves are of lesser importance – rather it is what the two families bring to the partnership that is important (Victorino-Soriano 2004). There is a strong obligation for young people to comply with the demands laid down by customary practice.

Marriage alliances are at the heart of Timorese culture (Molnar 2010). Irrespective of their age, once married the person is considered to be an adult, so marriage is a significant marker of adulthood. Typically rural girls are married when they are sexually mature, while boys are likely to marry when they are economically productive or independent. 'Girls marry at

14–18 years either because they are pregnant or their parents arrange it',[2] according to one female activist, while another noted the age of marriage for girls was typically during pre-secondary school and they are likely to be married to men seven to ten years older than themselves.[3] In a culture where age is a source of status, this difference in age further reinforces the superior status of the husband.

It is common practice to undertake both traditional and religious wedding ceremonies which may take place several years apart. At the traditional *adat*[4] marriage the settlement of the *barlake*,[5] a proscribed exchange of gifts between the family of the groom and the family of the bride, will bind the bride to the husband's family. The registration of marriage takes place through the church (Catholic, Protestant or Muslim clergy can register marriages) and the official church ceremony may not take place for some years. It is not uncommon for couples to already have children when the official church wedding takes place and the registration of marriage occurs. The Catholic Church only marries a couple after the traditional *barlake* negotiations are settled and these negotiations may be protracted.[6]

Traditionally marriage for a girl was arranged at puberty, but child marriage is now on the decline. However, cases of marriage as young as 10 are recorded, but the proportion of girls married by age 15 has declined from 7 percent amongst women now 40–44 years old, to 1 percent of women aged 15–19 years, in 2010 (NDS & UNFPA 2012). In 2010, ninety-two percent of female survey respondents between15–19 years old were never married, fifty-one percent were single at 24 years old and seventeen percent by 29 years old (NDS 2010:79). The median age of marriage has remained consistently around 20 years.

Married men are expected to participate, as responsible members of society, as decision makers, while women as wives and mothers are responsible for the household and domestic sphere. Young rural women often move directly from childhood to marriage, often lacking education or experience that could expand their knowledge. Parents exert control over girls' activities,

---

2   Interview Coordinator GFFTL, Dili 1 October 2005.

3   Interview, da Carvalho, Dili, 25 August 2006.

4   *Adat* means custom or tradition, the term deriving from Indonesian.

5   *Barlake* is the term used for the ritual exchange of goods between the bride's family and the groom's family. The groom's family gives the means of wealth creation, typically livestock which may be represented by several buffalo or as many as eighty buffalo in elite families in the district of Lautem, and the bride's family give an exchange gift of home production such as traditional woven cloth or *tais* and food products.

6   Interview, Director of the Teachers' Training College, Baucau, 18 August 2006.

explained as follows: 'Girls before marriage belong to the parents, thus have less right to decide. Boys belong to parents but have more rights if they go out, but not to bring back problems. But a girl might get pregnant'.[7] Familial concerns with the purity of girls, risks of pregnancy outside of marriage and potential loss of *barlake* are important issues for poor rural families, while individual rights have lower importance. In customary societies, a strong sense of obligation and reciprocal and mutual support places the community's interests at the apex of the moral order (Harris 2006). In spite of the strongly Catholicised culture, many women get pregnant before marriage. The reason, it was suggested, was that some young women exert a form of self-determination, getting pregnant to the man they choose, to force their family to accept the marriage and *barlake* offered so the marriage could go ahead quickly[8].

Silva has described how Portuguese colonial discourses have led to attitudes and observance of customary practices being stratified between the urbanised Timorese (*ema* Dili) and 'the people from the hills (*ema foho*)'. She further explains:

> If someone says that *barlake* is merely about 'buying' a wife, and hence a barbaric custom, s/he is presenting himself as a person from Dili (*ema* Dili), that is a modern/polite/civilised individual. On the other hand, one may say that *barlake* is a way of recognising the 'value' and the 'origins' of the bride and of her family as well as a toll for establishing alliances amongst families. By saying this, a person is presenting himself as an authentic East Timorese, someone who knows and honours his own traditions and understands the 'real' meaning of *barlake*; someone strongly connected to the hills (Silva 2011:152).

Young Timorese have varying positions on these issues. Some male activists argued that the *barlake* system is a major constraint on both education and development, because limited and precious family resources are siphoned away to meet customary obligations of ceremony and exchange.[9] This puts constraints on women, according to a Baucau activist:

> People spend more money on traditional ceremonies rather than on education. Marriage has a negative effect on education for children.

---

7   Interview, Covalima Youth Centre female staff, Suai, 16 September 2005.
8   Personal communication, Martins, Dili, 15 August 2006.
9   Interview Samala Rua, Dili, 31 July 2006.

> There is no improvement in your life because money is spent on *barlake*. Women are not involved in development partly due to politics and partly culture: parties do not choose women candidates for good positions as people consider that once women are married they should stay home.[10]

It was suggested that *barlake* limited the possibility of directing resources to education for family members or improved economic activities. In the coffee growing district of Ermera, which has the lowest level of literacy in the country, the practice of spending all the family income from coffee sales on *barlake*, wedding and funeral ceremonies is considered to be a cause of the particularly poor development indicators in that district. Following research and engagement on this issue by academics at the national university, local councils passed by-laws to put monetary limits on how much a family can spend in these ceremonies.[11]

The centrality of marriage customs to Timorese culture lead to gender differentiated attitudes towards education. Educating boys is seen as more important than girls because married men, except in the few matrilineal areas, stay on their cultural lands. When women move to their husbands' land (except in matrilineal societies) the value of her education is considered to be lost by her family. Young women explained that arranged marriages or pregnancy are a major cause of school dropout with many rural girls taken out of school in pre-secondary school (years 7–9) in order to marry, while some others are not permitted to travel the long distances from the villages to the post-primary schools.[12] As high schools are mostly located in the towns and nearly half of all secondary school students are in Dili, children often need to leave their village to attend school (Ministry of Education and Culture 2006:8). The numbers of girls attending primary school are almost equal to those of boys (Gender Parity Index: GPI 0.98), in pre-secondary (age 12–14) the attendance of girls is slightly higher than boys (GPI 1.02), but this is reversed with boys significantly outnumbering girls in secondary school (GPI 0.92) and tertiary studies (GPI 0.70) (NDS & UNFPA 2012:32–33). This limited participation in education by post-puberty females reflects the traditional and stereotyped view of roles of women and girls in the family and the community (Ministry of Education and Culture 2006:15). Although educational opportunities for girls are unequal, the change that

---

10 Interview, Community Education Foundation member, Baucau, 18 June 2006.
11 Personal communication, Mateus Tilman, Community Development Department, UNTL 10 August 2013.
12 Interviews: Abrantes, Dili 30 July 2006; Covalima Youth Centre staff, Suai, 16 September 2005.

has taken place is significant. Twenty-five percent of women completed pre-secondary or secondary school in 2010, compared to just eleven percent in 2004, and ninety-one percent of women over 60 years old have never been to school, though this figure is just eighteen percent for those 15–24 years (NDS & UNFPA 2012:34–35).

Gender-based Decision Making and Family Violence

Young women are encouraged to have children: a Timorese woman with a large number of children is considered senior to another with only one or two children and a wife who does not get pregnant every year may be subject to suspicion about her fidelity or fertility (Thatcher 1988). Child bearing starts immediately following marriage and Timorese women have large families. In 2007 Timor-Leste had the highest fertility rate in the world with an average of 7.8 children per woman, although 2010 figures suggested a drop in fertility rate to 5.7, and 62.5 percent of the population is under 24 years old (NDS 2010). More than two-thirds of Timorese women have become mothers by age 25 but there is little expressed desire by either men or women to have fewer children. Only 3.5 percent of women with one to three children and 9.4 percent of women with four or more children have used contraceptives (NDS 2010).

For a number of reasons the concept of family planning is not a priority for the majority of Timorese. First, children are highly valued and, as previously noted, having a large number of children grants a woman higher status. Second, most Timorese have lost family members during the occupation. During this time an estimated 200,000 Timorese died. Unsurprisingly there is a desire to rebuild their families. Third, Indonesian clinics ran a 'family planning program' based on forced sterilisation and forced use of injectable contraceptives or sterilisation.[13] This was strongly condemned by the Catholic Church. The Church's objection to both contraceptives and the Indonesian occupation has placed the use of contraception amid notions of oppression and sin. The church now promotes the 'natural rhythm method' of birth control, which requires acceptance and a degree of self-control by men, and it does not oppose condoms being promoted in HIV/AIDS education projects.[14] While many women have little control over their

---

13   In the late 1990s I heard many stories of women being forcibly sterilised or injected with Depo-Provera without their consent when they attended a government clinic or hospital. Consequently many Timorese were fearful of government clinics and would only attend Catholic clinics.

14   Interview Vicente, Suai 7 August 2006.

fertility, high maternal and infant mortality rates result from limited access to health services, the young age of mothers, the frequency of childbirth and poor health and nutrition of many mothers (Belton, Whittaker et al. 2009).

Sexual and reproductive health research has found that much effort is given to responding to reproductive needs, but there is less focus on providing necessary information and sexual services for youth, leaving adolescents vulnerable to sexual exploitation (Wayte, Zwi et al. 2008). The use of contraceptives by women prior to motherhood is negligible (NDS 2010). At the same time, young motherhood and frequent pregnancies leaves little time for young married women to participate fully in society through education, paid work or other activities outside the home (Wigglesworth 2009).

Gender relations in Timorese society dictate that the husband provides the house, food and money, and a wife is expected to do domestic duties, usually in the context of unequal power of decision making. A female activist explained how unequal power relations between men and women lead to domestic violence: 'men resolve problems with authority (including violence) while women are expected to remain silent and stay at home'.[15] A study of nearly 3000 women found thirty-eight percent of women had experienced violence since the age of 15 years, and twenty-nine percent experienced physical violence 'often' or 'sometimes' in the previous twelve months (NDS 2010). According to research with Timorese refugees in 1975, respondents claimed that in traditional marriages: 'the relationship is unequal because usually the wife belongs to her husband and his family and must always remain submissive to them' (Thatcher 1988:73).

In Covalima, where there is a high incidence of matrilineal social organisation, women are still required to listen to their husbands and accept and obey men's decisions. Research found that stability within the household is seen to be maintained where the wife is subordinate to the husband who is chief of the house and the key decision maker. Also a woman who expresses her views too much is likely to anger her husband, and risk a beating (Victorino-Soriano 2004).

Domestic violence is observed to be equally as common among the young couples of today as it was in previous generations; the young age of marriage and responsibility for children, together with the fact that young fathers have not established any mechanism for economic support, is blamed for heightened tensions between a couple that often lead to domestic violence.[16]

---

15   Interview Director of Rede Feto, Dili, 23 August 2006.
16   Personal communication, Martins, Dili, 15 August 2006.

Women who marry young are at significantly greater risk of violence by their partner, with low levels of education of the woman or her partner, and early marriage, also risk factors (Hynes, Ward et al. 2004). A staggering eighty-six percent of women believe that a husband is justified in beating his wife for reasons such as she goes out without telling him, she argues with him or she neglects the children (NDS 2010:214).

It has been suggested that children are beaten as a matter of habit, following values that young Timorese learnt in their own family life. At the launch of a UNICEF report into family violence in 2006, the Deputy Minister of Education and Culture explained that during the liberation struggle people became accustomed to living with violence, resulting in a particular 'culture of violence'. This results in domestic violence perpetrated by young men who repeat the behaviour of their parents.[17] This research found that sixty-seven percent of children in school had experienced their teacher beating them with a stick, while thirty-eight percent had been slapped on the face. More than half of all children had also experienced being beaten with a stick and shouted at by their parents (UNICEF 2006). Such expression through violence has also been said to arise from the patriarchal social structure, years of conflict and a militarised education during the Indonesian occupation which left many Timorese men with no other tools at their disposal (Myrttinen 2005). These portrayed masculinities have been actively constructed and need to be deconstructed through gender-sensitive strategies.

Since the passing of the Domestic Violence Law in 2010, the understanding of when physical abuse becomes 'domestic violence' and therefore subject to the Domestic Violence Law, has been subject to cultural interpretations. In a study of almost 500 young men, thirty percent of young men believed that it was okay for a man to beat his wife if the wife made a mistake, and sixty percent accepted a lower level of violence of a husband slapping or pushing their wives. The degree of acceptance of this behaviour increased as they got older and level of education had no discernible impact on this. The report noted that the education system currently does nothing to inhibit the trend of men developing aggressive masculine behaviours as they grow older (Wigglesworth, Niner et al. 2015). Further, national machinery (such as the LADV) have been put in place abruptly, without socialisation about the meaning of equality for men and women, that could have enabled citizens to accept and reconcile these changes with customary practices.

---

17   Launch of the 'Speak nicely to me – a study on practices and attitudes about discipline of children in Timor Leste', by UNICEF, Dili, 11 August 2006.

Struggle for Gender Equality in Timorese Civil Society

Timorese women started advocating for greater equality during the liberation struggle. FRETILIN's women's wing, Popular Women's Organisation of Timor (*Organisação Popular da Mulher de Timor* or OPMT), promoted the status of women amongst the political leadership of the resistance struggle and raised the political consciousness of women about the values of liberation, democracy and equality (Alves, Abrantes et al. 2003). These women challenged the Timorese traditions of polygamy and *barlake* which were outlawed by FRETILIN in the first *Manual Político* (political manual) in the mid-1970s (Aditjondro 2000:130).

Women played a crucial role in the clandestine movement at the organisational, political and logistical level and, as a result of their political work, many women were subjected to systematic sexual violence and rape by Indonesian soldiers (CAVR 2005). The clandestine movement was in fact composed of more than sixty percent women, who risked their lives to transport food to the guerrillas on the front line, or took up arms in the front lines themselves (Cristalis and Scott 2005:39). Yet while male heroes were recognised in the post-conflict era, no female combatants were included in the formal disarmament, demobilisation and reintegration programs (Thu, Scott et al. 2007).

FOKUPERS,[18] set up in 1997 to support women victims of violence, has since independence played a major role in bringing issues of domestic violence into the public arena. Women's organisations OPMT and Organisation of Timorese Women (OMT)[19] continue to operate, providing a grassroots network which enables the voices of rural women to be heard. *Rede Feto* was established in 2001 as a network of women's organisations as an outcome of the first National Women's Congress to present a united women's perspective in the political arena. It holds a Women's Congress every four years to bring together women from the districts and Dili to discuss women's issues. It has played a major role in advocating for a women's quota in parliament, resulting in the current requirement for political parties

---

18   FOKUPERS is the Indonesian acronym for East Timor Women's Communication Forum. It was the first independent women's NGO.

19   OPMT formed as FRETILIN's women's wing during the occupation, as mentioned previously. The *Organisação de Mulher Timorense* (OMT) was established as the women's wing of *Conselho National Resistencia Timorense* (CNRT) in 1998, which mirrored OPMT but embraced women from broader political affiliations within the pro-independence movement. Both organisations continue to exist.

to field one woman in each three party candidates. The NGO Women's Caucus was set up to support the process of promoting and supporting women candidates and arguing for their nomination amongst political parties (Trembath and Grenfell 2007).

Other women's NGOs include the Alola Foundation, established to nurture women leaders and advocate for the rights of women which and has played a significant role in promoting maternal and child health and early childhood education.[20] Young Women's Group of Timor-Leste (GFFTL),[21] supporting rural literacy and women's empowerment, and Strong Women Working Together (FKSH), focusing on women's livelihood projects,[22] were both set up by young women student activists, and both established working relationships with OMT to reach the grassroots level.

Apart from within these women-run NGOs, the opportunities for women in NGOs are limited, according to FONGTIL, the umbrella organisation of Timorese NGOs. Within Timorese civil society, FONGTIL has observed that typically women are found only in financial roles, a role traditionally ascribed to women, and in 'women's' activities such as health, education and gender issues (Wigglesworth and Soares 2006). Young women are notably in the minority in civil society organisations and progressive thinking about gender has not yet penetrated many Timorese civil society organisations.

Entrenched, unequal gendered attitudes have been described by female activists who believed that male activists do not want to encourage women in leadership. Indeed, interviews with male NGO leaders sometimes demonstrated either a lack of interest or a lack of appropriate strategies to address gender inequality (Wigglesworth 2009). Consequently, few women are visible in Timorese NGOs in the districts and educated women tend to concentrate in Dili where they can work as activists more freely and effectively.

Reluctance by local NGOs to question their own cultural practices exists because men in civil society, like others in society, internalise their cultural norms. In an internationally funded community development project in Latin America, it was found domestic violence cases were not taken to court because it was thought that women would be rejected from their communities for

---

20   Alola was established by then First Lady Kirsty Sword Gusmão in 2001 (see
     http://www.alola.org.au).

21   *Grupo Feto Foinsa'e Timor Lorosa'e* (GFFTL) was the women's wing of the student
     organisation ETSSC, which became a separate NGO after independence.

22   Young Women Working Together (*Feto Ki'ik Servico Hamutuk* – FKSH) was set up
     in 2004. It recently changed its name to *Feto iha Kbi'it Servico Hamutuk*, meaning
     'strong women working together', retaining the original acronym FKSH (see
     http://fkshtimorleste.org).

Gizela de Carvalho studied English and became a translator when the international community arrived in Dili. At the age of just 24 years, she set up her own organisation FKSH when the international NGO she worked with withdrew from Timor-Leste in 2004. Gizela continues as Director of FKSH which promotes economic empowerment of rural women. She is a key contributor to the National Women's Congress and is frequently invited to represent Timorese women at international conferences and meetings.

going against their spouses. Even forced child marriages in the communities were legitimised by NGOs as a cultural tradition in spite of the fact they were considered rape in law; legal rights were thus dismissed (Barrig 2007:123). NGOs did not question these cultural practices in the context of the law.

Timorese researcher, Josh Trindade, argues that men and women have complementary roles rather than a different status because they operate in different realms where feminine ritual power is protected by the 'outside' male political power, regulated by the *lulik* or spirit world. The argument sometimes heard in Timor-Leste, that gender issues are a foreign concept not appropriate to Timorese culture, fails to recognise the long-held convictions of Timorese women who have struggled for gender equality over decades. Activist women play a vital social role in this regard.

Empowerment for Women and Family Health

For women to be empowered, they must be given equal opportunity in development activities that will enable them to exert more control over their lives. Empowerment involves redressing unequal power relations and has been described as 'the expansion in people's ability to make strategic life choices in a context where this ability was previously denied to them' (Kabeer 1999:437). A measure of empowerment is the increased ability of the poor to make political, social or economic choices, related to three inter-related, indivisible but culturally determined dimensions: access to resources, agency to define one's goals and act on them, and self-assessed achievements in the process of empowerment (Kabeer 1999).

Historically, gender issues have been overlooked, as the household has been understood as a basic unit of economic measure with a male head of household. Women's interests were completely overlooked in development programming until Ester Boserup first drew attention to the fact that most African farmers were women, and women were often disadvantaged by agricultural development interventions (Boserup 1970). The reality is that women in most poor countries play a major role in agricultural production but are often seen by policy makers just as wives and mothers (Jaquette and Staudt 2007:24). 'Women in development' interventions at this time were based on the concept that it was more 'efficient' to engage the female fifty percent of the population in productive activities to make economic development more efficient, rather than giving attention to gender inequities (Ostergaard 1992; Parpart 1995). Some useful conceptual tools were developed to analyse gender relationships and work-loads.

Critics argued that a key issue for women was the unequal balance of power between men and women and overcoming the disadvantage which results in women making up seventy percent of the world's poorest. A focus on 'gender' rather than 'women' in the late 1980s aimed to promote strategies aimed at changing the gender relationships that defined women's roles and subordinate position (Moser 1991). Highlighting women's 'triple burden' of being responsible for the productive role of food production, domestic or reproductive responsibilities of cooking, washing, collecting water and firewood, caring for the children and child bearing, as well as fulfilling roles and obligations with respect to community activities, Moser argued that unpaid domestic labour and the community responsibilities that comprise a large part of women's social obligations are not valued. Men's work on the other hand is valued because it is generally remunerated and carries with it some measure of social status or political power (Moser 1991).

The market economic policies were found to further impact on women as privatisation and reduced public services led to increasing burdens on women to provide for the family (Kabeer 1994). Already overloaded with domestic tasks and community roles, women were expected to also make and sell produce to raise cash for the newly imposed school fees and health expenses for their children, making women victims of neo-liberal economic policies (Jaquette and Staudt 2007).

Empowerment of women requires recognising and striving to overcome the disadvantage that their gender confers and supporting women by removing obstacles from their path and giving encouragement to take charge of their lives (Blackburn 2004:220). Gender mainstreaming policies are now promoted across development institutions to ensure gender equality exists across all aspects of organisational and public policy. Timor-Leste has adopted a gender mainstreaming approach, as have many of the major aid and development organisations that support it. Often the implementation of these strategies has not lived up to its ideal. Sometimes gender mainstreaming has been found lacking due to the failure of the institution to internalise gender equality measures by donor agency management and staff (Jaquette and Staudt 2007:38). Other times activities are directed towards women's 'feminine' role (such as caring for small animals and home gardens) as a result of passive if not overt resistance in the cultural context in which they operate (Barrig 2007:130). Yet, the importance of women's participation in economic, social and community development was highlighted by Kofi Annan, former Secretary General of the UN, in his speech on International Women's Day 2005:

> Study after study has taught us that there is no tool for development more effective than the empowerment of women. No other policy is as likely to raise economic productivity, or to reduce infant and maternal mortality. No other policy is as sure to improve nutrition and promote health – including the prevention of HIV/AIDS. No other policy is as powerful in increasing the chances of education for the next generation. And I would venture that no policy is more important in preventing conflict or in achieving reconciliation after a conflict has ended.[23]

One of the most intractable indicators of poverty in Timor-Leste, child malnutrition, could be addressed through women's empowerment. Globally, evidence suggests that women's empowerment is the most effective

---

23   www.un.org/News/ossg/sg/stories/AnnanKeySpeeches.asp.

way to achieve improved family health. The Health and Demographic Survey of 2009–10 shows that 58 percent of Timorese children are stunted and suffer from malnutrition, whilst a massive 19 percent of children are severely affected by malnutrition. Women, particularly young mothers, need the ability to decide which crops will be produced on the family plot, knowledge of how to put more nutritional food on the table, and greater control over their reproductive health.

Timor-Leste's customary practices dictate women's work defined by the domestic sphere, and as men are the principle decision makers, women are expected to 'stay home and be silent'.[24] This negatively impacts on expectations by and of women in relation to their participation in development projects, such as committees, user groups, or community action groups. This can reproduce and exacerbate existing forms of exclusion, for example existing community power structures used in international development projects may result in the traditional male leadership becoming the key or only source of contact (Mosse 2001). While participatory processes are intended to involve and listen to 'the community', women, who lack time and may not necessarily be accepted in community decision-making forums, may not be represented. It is suggested these processes have the potential to benefit women only if practitioners of participatory methods first address gender power relations in the community (Crawley 1998). The question of who participates and who benefits are critical questions, as the voices of the more marginal may barely be raised, let alone heard in these spaces, argues Cornwall (2003). Women may be said to have 'participated' simply because demands have been made on them to supply physical labour necessary for the implementation of a project, or because they have sat quietly in a meeting without making their views heard.

Due to the limitations on women in rural society, many young rural women who obtain a secondary or tertiary education do not want to return to the rural areas. Today's young women seek to escape the hold of tradition after completing higher education, by getting a job or seeking a husband in the urban areas.[25] Others return from overseas study to reject the idea of being 'exchanged for buffalo'.[26] Traditionally most women did not work outside the home; for example, before independence nurses and teachers were predominantly male. Due to changing gender expectations, by 2006

---

24 Interview with Director of Rede Feto, Dili, 23 August 2006.
25 Interviews, Coordinator GFFTL Dili 1 October 2005; Covalima Youth Centre staff, Suai, 16 September 2005.
26 Interview; UNDIL lecturer, Dili, 25 September 2005.

women made up an impressive 76 out of 113 applicants to the Catholic Teachers College,[27] and by 2012 women made up 20 percent of the country's police service.[28] This suggests a significant change in expectations among some members of the younger generation. Young women are more visible as leaders within civil society groups than previously. In 2006 one young woman was elected from among her predominantly male peers as coordinator of their youth theatre group in Baucau[29] and another was similarly chosen as the coordinator of the youth group in her *bairro* in Dili.[30] The idea that young women can be leaders appears to be more prevalent among younger men and women.

Perhaps the strongest symbol of change concerning the participation of women in contemporary Timor-Leste is the number of women in senior office. The Fifth Constitutional Government included twenty-four women of the sixty-five members (38 percent) of the National Parliament, giving Timor-Leste the highest proportion of female parliamentary representatives in Southeast Asia. There were also two women ministers (ministers for Finance and Social Solidarity) and three vice-ministers (two in Health and one in Education) in the Fifth Government.

Summary

Both gender and rural-urban differences have impacted on people's experience of 'development'. In Timor-Leste, kinship alliances bound by marriage are at the heart of Timorese culture and carry expectations that Timorese women will fulfil domestic and subservient roles. However there has been a long-standing campaign for greater gender equality and, although these traditions limit the opportunities for young women, many seek to broaden their engagement through community activities or civil society organisations. In Dili, Timorese women have successfully establish-ed various NGOs that are addressing and changing gender norms, but in rural areas change is slow and more difficult for women to realise. A high level of female participation in national government stands in stark contrast to the rural situation. As more young rural women achieve higher levels of education, however, they may be in a position to challenge the prevailing social norms to promote more gender equitable approaches.

27   Interview with Director of the Teachers' Training College, Baucau, 18 June 2006.
28   UN Secretary General's address to Timorese parliament on 15 August 2012.
29   Interview with Buka Hatene theatre group, Baucau, 18 August 2006.
30   Interview, Coordinator of Humanitarian Study Club, Dili, 21 August 2006.

Chapter Five

YOUTH, CONFLICT AND URBANISATION

Large scale international interventions can create a differential in the well-being of the rural and urban communities, reflecting where international funds flow and work opportunities are concentrated. Dili has become a magnet for young people seeking alternatives to the hard life of a subsistence farmer. Young school leavers have flocked to the bright lights of the city for a 'modern' lifestyle but many have become unemployed. Causes of the political crisis which broke out in 2006, the vulnerability of youth to being attracted into gangs driven by disaffected groups and civil society engagement are discussed.

Youth Migration for Work

Ordinary rural families had access to education for the first time under the Indonesian regime, so young graduates were often proudly the first educated members of their families. On completing primary school, rural children typically had to leave home to attend pre-secondary school. If families did not have relatives near the school other arrangements were made. Some students started living independently at the age of thirteen, building a house in the district town with their village peers. At this early age they looked after themselves, including handling shopping, cooking and firewood collection, with the help of money they received each week when their parents came to the Saturday market to sell farm produce.[1] Children studying away from home could thus have a high degree of independence, or be living with and dependent on distant family members.

In Timor-Leste, there are high expectations amongst those who have attended school with the idea of 'employment' strongly linked to working in a government office. The government service employs half the number of staff

---

1   Interviews, Barros, Suai, 7 August 2006; Vicente, Suai, 7 August 2006.

as during the Indonesian administration, but the number of school leavers seeking jobs has escalated. There is an expectation by youth and their parents that education will provide a better life for their children than the marginal subsistence of previous generations. School fees are paid in expectation of a return, for example that their child will recompense this by bringing an income into the family. Some rural parents have demanded that their educated children bring money into the family from paid work, not realising that their children's level of education is minimal and work is scarce.[2] In the rural areas there are few formal employment opportunities available, while agricultural work and other forms of casual paid work are often excluded from people's concept of being employed (Ostergaard 2005:28). Youth migration to the towns also has resulted in some rural communities suffering from lack of labour for farming (Wigglesworth 2007).

In Timor-Leste, each year about 17,000 young people enter the labour force.[3] In 2010 the Timorese economy was only able to provide approximately 400 new jobs in the private sector (RDTL 2011:111). Driving taxis or running minibuses is a major income generation activity for young Timorese with few skills, but it is not considered exactly 'employment' by youth, but as temporary, transitional work whilst awaiting the desired office job.[4] This experience is not unique to Timor-Leste, but studies have shown that a significant cause of conflict amongst youth is their unmet and unrealistic aspirations for white collar work when they leave school, in places as diverse as Sri Lanka and the Solomon Islands (Gunawardena 2002; AusAID 2003).

Dili draws in young people due to its large number of educational establishments, job opportunities and urban lifestyle. Transitioning from a rural lifestyle under the influence of customary leaders to that of the urban culture was fuelled by a desire for a different life, according to a youth leader:

> Urban drift is because they want a better life. Land does not generate regular income. There are no secondary schools in the village so they move to the district or Dili. Some come for fun life in the city. Their expectation is that the city has opportunities to get money.[5]

Young Timorese who have moved to urban centres experience a very different environment to that they left behind in the rural areas. Local chiefs

2   Interview, Coordinator of District Youth Council, Suai, 4 August 2006.
3   Timor-Leste National Youth Employment Action Plan 2009, SEFOPE, Dili.
4   Interview with DIT Student Association leader, 8 September 2005.
5   Interview Samala Rua, Dili, 31 July 2006.

appointed in the urban *bairros* do not have the same authority over youth as traditional chiefs in rural areas:

> Traditional leaders are important in decision making and cultural activities and young people have a close relation to traditional leaders, whereas political leaders are respected but distant. In urban areas political leaders become important and traditional practices are reduced.[6]

The consequence of this is that many youth seek alternative forms of social connection through peer-group activities, and seek an identity on the basis of kinship, political or martial arts affiliations, or fashion: 'Most youth try to move away from tradition, they like fashion, to follow trends for clothes and haircuts, street life and an office job'.[7]

Youth who made the trip to Dili looking for work had often left junior or senior high school with limited skills. The Youth Survey found that although 75 percent of youth had attended nine years of schooling, only 66 percent were functionally literate (SSYS & UNICEF 2005). In 2006 it was estimated that youth made up a third of the population of Dili, including job seekers and school and university students (Curtain 2006). The National Youth Survey commissioned by SSYS and UNICEF surveyed 15–35 year olds across six of the thirteen districts of Timor-Leste as well high school and university students in Dili (Curtain and Taylor 2005).[8] It found that nine out of ten rural youth believed they had an important role in their communities and that most under-thirty-five year olds believed their access to education and economic prospects, as well as quality of home dwelling and environmental health, were better than was the case for their parents. There was a sense of security from violence and crime and confidence that the government understood, and would act on, the problems facing youth (SSYS & UNICEF 2005). This study was produced just months prior to the crisis of 2006.

In 2006 in Timor-Leste, groups of young men with no gainful employment congregated in the streets, while young women were engaged in family domestic duties. 'Since independence the situation has been very bad for youth … even youth who have skills do nothing so their skills will

---

6   Interview Samala Rua, Dili, 31 July 2006.
7   Interview Lemos, Dili, 11 August 2006.
8   A random sample of twenty-five villages across six districts plus 300 young people from four high schools outside of Dili, four within Dili, and two universities, with thirty students from each institution incorporating equal numbers of males and females in a sample of 780 young people.

be lost,"[9] complained a youth in a district town. Following the 2006 crisis there was much emphasis on establishing youth for work programs and on building youth skills by engagement in community construction projects. These activities did not resolve the shortage of employment opportunities in the long term for semi-literate and low skilled students annually discharged from educational establishments. Many school leavers continued to idle away their time in the streets. Public discourse focussed on levels of unemployment, often misreported and exaggerated, and failed to address the reality of different kinds of work that may be imagined or obtainable. The migration to Europe for work has increased, with youth with Portuguese grandparents benefiting from access to a European Union passport to get work in Britain or Ireland. A nationally orchestrated work program sent a thousand youths to work in South Korea in factories and construction work (RDTL 2006). In a country that is unlikely to provide many jobs in the formal sector for many years to come, the importance of youth involvement in the informal economy has been inadequately supported. Even the World Bank has now included subsistence farming and self-employment in its definition of jobs: 'Jobs are performed by the employed. These are defined as people who produce goods and services for the market or for their own use' (World Bank 2013:5).

Before the 2006 crisis in Dili, there was little attention given to youth, but following the crisis senior government officials were describing young men in language such as 'hooligans', 'rampaging youth', 'thugs', and 'vandals', demonising all youth even though only a minority become involved in such activities (Walsh 2006). As in Timor-Leste, youth in South Africa were on the frontline of the liberation struggle and it has been found that youth who lived through the conflict often slipped back into violent behaviour when, as a result of peace, they lost their former roles and were not supported (Marks 2001). After the ban on the ANC was lifted, the failure of political leadership to engage the youth movements in the new political environment led to an increasing incidence of unorganised violence and crime (Marks 2001). Similarly, insufficient attention was given to integrating young people from the armed struggle into society in Mozambique, where it is claimed their engagement in violent crime resulted from the high incidence of depression and aggressiveness of former young soldiers (Aird, Etraime et al. 2001). The media can be quick to highlight youth violence and crime, creating a negative image of youth, and the media in South Africa have been

---

9   Youth art group leader, Manatuto, interview, Dili, 22 August 2006.

blamed for focussing on youth as a 'lost generation' or 'the problem' while failing to highlight the environment that created social divisions in the first instance (Seekings 1996).

Youth unemployment has been a perennial concern of governments worldwide in relation to issues of social control. This concern pivots on a fear that if a sense of achievement is absent for youth, they may seek self-validation through criminality or violence (Ansell 2005). Often, and arguably this is the case in Timor-Leste, it is only when youth become a 'problem' that are they are given due attention. Indeed much of the literature on youth is about youth violence and crime, with the study of youth being linked to the field of criminology, in contrast to the study of children which emerged from developmental psychology (Ansell 2005:15). In the Pacific the concentration of development aid to support the capacity of the central government left the countryside depleted of energetic, skilled and innovative individuals who could enable development in rural areas (Connell 2002:53). Meanwhile, youth disengagement in urban areas of New Guinea led to violent crime known as 'raskolism', with law and order responses are said to be contributing to the problem of violence. Some organisations are promoting traditional customs as a way to find solutions (Howley 2005; Regan 2005).

In Timor-Leste in 2006 youth leaders spoke of how youth prepared proposals for agricultural projects, music groups and sporting activities, but were not able to obtain funding for any of these initiatives and programs.[10] Youth activists had been consulted by the government in the preparation of the national youth policy but they lamented the lack of activity or progress since that time. In Dili, one activist argued: 'The government has not given any funds to youth groups to develop their own capacity. Only talk, no implementation, so young people feel marginalised'.[11]

The limited opportunities for young people resulted in many youth in rural towns 'hanging around', playing guitars, drinking or gambling. 'Young people are just sitting in the road with no job', lamented a twenty-four year old woman activist from Baucau in 2006,[12] while another believed an increase in drinking, gambling and fighting by youth stemmed from a sense of loss and alienation:

> When I work with young people more people say they have lost their future. They do not know how they can live for the future. The situation

---

10   Interview, Coordinator District Youth Council, Suai, 4 August 2006.
11   Interview, Gusmão Soares, Dili, 29 July 2006.
12   Female leader of youth group, interview, Baucau, 18 August 2006.

has reduced the human ability. They don't know what their vision is. The public education is very low quality – when young people leave school they are not doing anything, only stay around the house and gather food from the farm. If they don't go to the field they only stay drinking. It is a problem when they drink sometimes they start fighting and become violent.[13]

Drinking and drug use were mentioned as increasing social problems and attributed to the fact that there is not only unemployment, but also few other activities for youth. Drinking and drug use were said to have increased since 2005 when the Youth Social Analysis study recorded little use of drugs. By 2006 drugs were frequently used and it was believed by some that these had been brought into the country to fuel the violence.[14] Unemployed young men became the front line of the crisis which started in February 2006 and continued to February 2008.

Expectations, Disappointments and Conflict

In 2006, there was a pervasive sentiment within the population that the expectation of freedom and development for which they had made sacrifices had not been realised. In the early years of independence, people's experience was contrary to their expectation, with declining standards of living contributing to the alienation of many rural communities as poverty in the rural areas rose while power and resources were concentrated in Dili. The Ministry of Finance showed that poverty had increased between 2001 and 2007, causing a real decline in per-capita consumption by 26 percent, in spite of the huge volumes of aid which were flowing into the country (NDS 2008). The significant increase in poverty was explained by the stagnation of the non-oil economy between 2001 and 2007, which declined by 12 percent over this period.[15]

Amongst Timor-Leste's largest ethno-linguistic group, the *Mambai*, there was a belief that justice should result in some redistribution of material and symbolic assets on the basis of contribution to the liberation struggle (Traube 2007). Traube argued that *Mambai* people living predominantly in the poorest highlands districts perceived that their sacrifices for the

---

13   Catholic youth group leader, interview, Baucau, 19 August 2006.
14   Interview with Youth Social Analysis research team member, 31 July 2006.
15   Press release on 'Timor-Leste: Poverty in a Young Nation' report launched 26 November 2008. The report is based on the Timor-Leste Standard of Living Study 2007.

independence struggle had not been recognised or compensated following the establishment of the state. At independence former FALINTIL troops were demobilised and had to return to subsistence farming in order to survive. Many youth had sacrificed their opportunity for education to take up arms at a young age, and after independence some were resentful at returning to subsistence communities because they had never farmed before. An activist explained the sentiment:

> Most of our generation are farmers now. They did not get a good education. These youth think government should create a job suitable for them, at least labour work. We involved in the clandestine movement expect something from government.[16]

An ex-FALINTIL guerrilla from the east of the country received just three years of Portuguese primary schooling before he joined the freedom fighters in 1976, dedicating twenty-three years of his life to the armed struggle. On demobilisation he received just US$350, after which he was on his own, looking for the means to survive.[17] A former FALINTIL guerrilla leader, from the west of the country, complained: 'The government is not looking to the people, especially veterans. Many people died and much suffering but the government doesn't have any program to support them'.[18] There have been targeted programs to support ex-freedom fighters. For instance the International Organisation of Migration (IOM) had a substantial program of support for veterans. But it only operated in the eastern districts. Other programs have also been selective in their targets, leaving many veterans unable to access support.[19] By 2006, that the government had not given recognition to the contribution and suffering of the resistance fighters, or

---

16   Interview, Barreto, Suai, 8 August 2006.
17   Personal communication 17 August 2006. He could not name the organisation that provided support.
18   Interview with a former regional leader of FALINTIL, Suai, 8 August 2006. Although the term 'veterans' is in popular use, according to the Commission of the Combatants in the Resistance '*Veteranos*' (veterans) refers to those who served in FALINTIL for the whole period 1975–1999, of whom there are only seventy-five persons. Other former freedom fighters are technically known as the '*antigos combatants*' (former combatants) who fought with arms during some of that period. The '*Quadros de resistencia*' (members of resistance organisations) includes civilians who supported the resistance, notably the youth organisations OJETIL, RENETIL, FITUN, OBJLATIL etc.
19   One example is Project RESPECT set up by UNDP to support social and economic reintegration of ex-combatants, widows and unemployed youth into civilian life. Project Respect was critiqued by NGO La'o Hamutuk for allocating only just over US$1 million to local activities in a US$13 million project (La'o Hamutuk 2004).

delivered material improvement to their lives, became a major source of bitterness, particularly with plentiful resources clearly visible in the capital.

Disenfranchisement resulted because the independent government failed to deliver benefits to the population in the form of improved health, education and support to farmers. This was expected as a result of the government working on their behalf, as opposed to the former Indonesian and Portuguese regimes. People perceived government actions as inimical to their interests when the effects of reduced support in agriculture and declining opportunities for marketing of agricultural produce started to be felt. There were criticisms that the government did not consult the people or listen to the concerns and needs of Timorese citizens.[20] In 2005 a three-week long demonstration initiated by the Catholic Church resulted in the country being almost brought to a standstill and the first call for the Prime Minister, Mari Alkatiri, to resign. A former military adviser believed the role of veterans in the country 'dominates the community's political equation from the village to the capital' (Rees 2003:1).

In February 2006, 591 soldiers from the western districts had deserted their barracks in protest at perceived discrimination against westerners within the military and were sacked by Taur Matan Ruak, Commander of the armed forces (F-FDTL). The sacked soldiers represented almost the entire contingent of soldiers from the western districts, who accused senior officers of F-FDTL of claiming that the Timorese from eastern districts (*Lorosa'e*) were responsible for winning the liberation struggle, implying westerners were pro-integrationists, and overlooking westerners for promotion, amongst other concerns.[21] President Gusmão returned from an overseas trip to make a televised address in which he acknowledged the injustice of the decision and the existence of east–west discrimination in the military. He also declared that he would not reverse the decision.[22] That night the first acts of communal violence broke out, resulting from clashes between *Lorosa'e* (eastern) and *Loromuno* (western) youth gangs. Within days, youths were involved in widespread looting and burning of houses in Dili. According to Timorese activists, by legitimising the grievances

---

20   Interview, Barros, Suai, 7 August 2006.
21   *Loromuno* (from the land of the setting sun) and *LoroSa'e* (from the land of the rising sun) is the Tetum version of east and west). Senior military officials had dismissed the grievances presented to them, without a military tribunal, claiming that political opposition parties were behind the protest.
22   Speech of President Xanana Gusmão on 23 March 2006 at the Palace of Ashes, Dili. http://en.wikisource.org/wiki/Palace_of_Ashes,_Speech_Xanana_Gusm%C3%A3o,_23th_March_2006 (viewed 13 February 2007).

of 'westerners' the President's speech had provoked attacks on 'easterners'. Within a few days, seventeen homes had been burned and easterners were fleeing the city (International Crisis Group 2006:8).

The crisis escalated when, on 23 May, the army (FALINTIL-*Forcas de Defensa de Timor-Leste*, F-FDTL) and police force (*Policia Nacional de Timor-Leste*, PNTL) turned on each other. Foreign troops were called in to restore order. Violence in the streets, mostly perpetrated by gangs of young men, identified as being from the east (*Lorosa'e*) or the west (*Loromuno*) continued during 2006 and into 2007. The youth denied responsibility, blaming the '*ema bo'ot*' ('big people', or leaders) for their actions and some claimed to have been enticed with money (Scambary 2006; Grove N et al. 2007).

The armed forces – F-FDTL – are historically linked with FRETILIN and the resistance fighters, while the PNTL, directed by the Ministry of the Interior, was formed by UNTAET, with many police officers from the western districts who had previously served the Indonesian administration. The new head of the police force (PNTL) was a police officer during the Indonesian administration. UNTAET vetted and rehired any police who had worked for the Indonesian government even though they were locally perceived as pro-integrationists. Significant donor resources supported the development of the police force, including through training of police officers provided by the Australian Federal Police and Australian aid.[23] International donors were not able to provide 'development aid' to F-FDTL because military assistance is excluded from the OECD definition of development assistance. Only 650 of the former resistance fighters were recruited into the 1500 strong F-FDTL, thereby excluding the majority of FALINTIL guerrillas, heroes of the liberation struggle (Rees 2003; Peake 2013). This simple beginning escalated into a political and military crisis that brought the country to its knees for two years. In June 2006 Alkatiri was forced to step down as Prime Minister, to be replaced by Jose Ramos Horta until national elections were held in 2007. According to Scambary, expectations of the situation stabilising as a result of Prime Minister Alkatiri's resignation were dashed as new phases of violence developed, involving a new set of actors (Scambary 2007). While the first phase of violence had involved clashes between the security forces and anti-government demonstrations, the second phase involved protracted street brawls between ethnically

---

23   The Australia-East Timor Police Development Program, worth A\$32 million, has trained over 800 staff within East Timor's police service (www.ausaid.gov.au/country/ cbrief.cfm?DCon=5901_3683_7838_3843_6784&CountryID=911&Region=EastAs ia, accessed 27 November 2008).

based groups, and a third phase evolved through conflicts between former clandestine cells and martial arts groups (Scambary 2007).

By July 2006 half the population of Dili was living in refugee camps. This was a major social crisis requiring a humanitarian response by development agencies. The crisis continued into mid-2007, paralysing or reversing many of the development gains of previous years. In the April 2007 elections Jose Ramos Horta was elected as President, with the Parliamentary elections in June resulting in Xanana Gusmão becoming Prime Minister.[24] The Gusmão government took a high spending approach, benefitting from the substantial oil revenues that began flowing in 2005 and which enabled a massive increase in the national budget to resource programs aimed at resolving problems created by the crisis, including providing pensions to the veterans.[25]

The hostilities between east and west are worth examining here, as they created real fears of the disintegration of Timor-Leste as a united country.[26] There is no single ethnic divide between the east and west, rather there are multiple linguistic groups with some distinct characteristics. The Timorese languages are largely of Austro-Malay roots, although three language groups have Papuan roots (Makassae and Fataluku in the east, and Bunak in the west). The Portuguese colonisers played on the differences between language groups, naming those in the longer pacified western districts the *kaladi* or 'quiet ones', while the more distant and warrior-like easterners were termed *firaku* or 'those that turn their back on you' (Carey 2007). The empirical histories of struggle by the Timorese against Portuguese rule, however, suggest these namings did not always correspond to the reality. According to Freitas, during the colonial period most revolts against the Portuguese authorities took place in the west of East Timor, while people from the eastern kingdoms that had accepted Portuguese rule were recruited to fight alongside Portuguese troops to put down uprisings in the west (Freitas

---

24 Xanana Gusmão had stepped down as President in order to form a separate party to contest FRETILIN in the national elections. During this period a third interim government was formed which ran from the April 2007 until the formation of a new government after the parliamentary elections on 30 June 2007. FRETILIN received the largest vote but lacked a clear majority. Agreement could not be reached on the leadership, resulting in a political deadlock until President Ramos Horta finally called on Xanana Gusmão to form government in a coalition with the minority parties. Gusmão became the Prime Minister of what is named the Fourth Constitutional Government in August 2007.

25 Lindsay Murdoch, 'Timor Collides with its future', *The Age*, Melbourne 22 November 2008.

26 For instance a Ten District Movement formed under the leadership of Major Tara. The ten of thirteen districts represent the westerners, but excluded the eastern districts Baucau, Viqueque and Los Palos (International Crisis Group 2006).

1994:10). Nevertheless, a 'western' Timorese activist explained that as school students they were encouraged to choose an easterner (a fighter) when they had to select their sports team captain, highlighting the common perception of the fiercer characteristics of the easterners.[27]

A Timorese academic explained that prior to 2006, the term *Loromuno* was generally used to refer to people from Indonesian West Timor. However, back in 1975 Hill made reference to these terms, noting that 'one of the variations of tribalism is the division of the population in *Loro Muno* and *Loro Sa'e*, into *Kaladis* and *Firakus* … and the belief that some groups are superior to others' (Hill 2002:77). The senior officers of FALANTIL, and more recently F-FDTL, were from the east. As the majority of the militia groups were based in the west, close to the border with Indonesia, senior officers have indiscriminately accused *Loromuno* members of being pro-integrationist. The sense of superiority of senior *Lorosa'e* military officers is evidenced by their claim that the *Lorosa'e* alone were responsible for winning the liberation struggle (see Peake 2013:67).

As well, rivalry between the Makassae from the east and the Bunak from the west over market supremacy dates back to an influx of easterners into the capital after World War Two,[28] and these tensions resumed after further population displacement caused another influx into Dili in 1999 (Babo-Soares 2003). The Bunak are a relatively small language group, but the Makassae,[29] who became major players in Dili markets, are one of the largest language groups and are perceived as a threat by some Dili market stall holders.[30]

Behind this issue of ethnicity, a primary cause of violence in both Dili and the districts was family land and property disputes, many dating back to overlapping claims from Portuguese or Indonesian times (Brady and Timberman 2006). Unresolved land ownership disputes sometimes arose from pro and anti-integration sentiment and population movements in 1999 or were linked to political divisions which started in 1975. Within Timor-Leste successive waves of people were displaced and forced to move as a result of armed conflict and Indonesian policies of occupation. There was forcible

---

27   Personal communication, Martins, Dili, 15 August 2006.
28   Ranck suggests the influx into Dili took place in 1959. 'Recent rural-urban migration to Dili, Portuguese Timor'. MA Thesis, 1977, Macquarie University.
29   The Makassae are principally from the Baucau district, and the Bunak are one of the two principle language groups in Covalima and also from Bobonaro district. According to the Timor-Leste Survey of Living Standards 2007, Mambai make up 24.6%, Tetum Praca 17.4%, Tetum Terik 6.3%, Makassae 11.7% and Bunak are 5.7% of the population (National Directorate of Statistics 2007). Interestingly Bunak is the only language of the Papuan group found in the west of the country.
30   Personal communication, Martins, Dili, 15 August 2006.

removal of villages away from FRETILIN occupied mountains, large tracts of land in the coastal plains were allocated to Indonesian transmigrants and, in 1999, huge displacement resulted from the violence unleashed by the Indonesian backed militia. Land ownership is therefore a highly contentious issue, with titles from Portuguese and Indonesian periods each having validity. Many landowners who fled after 1975 have returned to claim their property, now home to other families. And numerous families arrived in Dili to escape violence in 1999 and did not leave again. Houses vacated by the departing Indonesians were reoccupied. Numerous ownership claims have been lodged, but the judicial system has as yet not responded to these claims. With thousands of land and property ownership claims pending over many years, it is argued that most property destruction was aimed at those who had moved into homes of others in the post-1999 era. Lists of properties occupied since 1999 were sometimes obtained from hamlet heads to target them more efficiently (McWilliam 2007:41). The media reported that youth were found with wads of money after being paid to burn specific houses.[31] In the 2006 crisis the burning of houses to dislodge the occupants appears to have been a specific action designed to forcibly resolve property issues. Violence in the streets ultimately caused half the population of Dili to retreat to makeshift refugee camps scattered around the capital.

Masculinity, Groups and Gangs

Activists claimed lack of direction and orientation of young men as a factor in the crisis: 'Youth became involved only after things had happened because there had been no direction to guide them. They are looking for identity and not thinking of the impact on the community'[32]. Many youth involved in the violence claimed they were manipulated, that leaders had distributed weapons and stirred up hatred with divisive words about East and West. Activists also commented on the responsibility of the leadership for the youth violence:

> Youth with low education cannot analyse well the positive and negative side. It is easy to manipulate them as they easily follow people who want to make violence.[33]

---

31   A Catholic priest stated that youth claim to receive $20 for throwing stones; $50 for burning a house and $100 for killing a person. He received this information in confessions of dozens of youths (Marianne Kearney, *Courier Mail* 9 October 2007).
32   Interview, Samala Rua, Dili, 31 July 2006.
33   Interview, de Carvalho, Dili, 25 August 2006.

> Young people do not understand politics. Political leaders are behind young people's actions.[34]

INGO staff working with youth in the IDP camps reported that young men blamed the violence on '*ema bot*' (big people) even though they themselves committed the violent acts. Some were enticed with money: 'Leaders gave money to young people. For money people will do anything, even kill' said one youth (Grove N et al. 2007:9). Gang members gained courage and reputedly money to undertake acts of violence that they had not done before. On the other hand, many youths engaged in violence without financial reward due to their frustration of being unemployed: 'Young people are concerned about what *Ema Bot* are saying. They are only involved in violence because they are made to. They are not paid. They are involved in violence to express their frustration and disappointment'.[35]

The explosive mix of poorly educated unemployed male youth within a highly volatile politicised environment resulted in youth gangs obeying leaders who 'made' them carry out violent acts. Research found that youth blamed their leaders, often former leaders of the resistance movement (Scambary 2006), while few youth would admit to being responsible for the violence.[36] Some young men directly blamed then President Gusmão for the start of the crisis: 'The careless words of leaders incited violence; that accusations of not having fought for independence forced people to fight and defend their name and their self-worth' (Grove N et al. 2007:3).

Youth admitted they had been used by other organisations, some political parties. 'It is the culture of "*Maun Bo'ot*" (big brother). If "*Maun Bo'ot*" said to do something, after a few beers they can do anything', reported a youth researcher.[37] The Baucau District Administrator reflected that a 'culture of violence' existed because many youth growing up during the struggle lacked nurturing and 'learnt to burn houses' and engage in anti-social behaviour.[38] In addition to the background of violence in their lives, the culture encourages a manly response: 'Parents give "*carinho*" (affection) to girls but not to boys'.[39] The lived experiences of many youth contributed to social dislocation and the willingness to engage in violence. That the leaders of youth gangs engaged in looting and burning across Dili is perhaps an

---

34   Interview, Gusmão Soares, Dili, 29 July 2006.
35   Interview, Catholic Youth Coordinator, Dili, 15 August 2006.
36   Personal communication with James Scambary, 24 August 2006.
37   Interview with youth researcher 31 July 2006.
38   Interview District Administrator, Baucau, 17 August 2006.
39   Interview, Abrantes, Dili, 30 July 2006.

indication of youth's continued uncritical acceptance of authority. In the words of a Timorese academic: 'the culture of youth is to respect a leader even if they are wrong'.[40]

Much of the 2006 violence resulted from family disputes dating back to 1975. Political or resistance leaders drew on the resentment and disappointment of young people to carry out their family battles and political aspirations. Some groups were involved in extortion rackets and criminal gangs, others had affiliations to former militia groups while others were linked to senior members of government (Scambary 2006). Politicisation of the conflict is not attributed to political parties, rather it was driven by community-level rivalries: 'If political manipulation did occur, it was most likely at the village or neighbourhood level and individual and fraternal linkages rather than strategic campaigns organised and executed nationally' (Arnold 2009:387).

The perpetrators of youth violence were largely from the 'millennium generation' brought up in the 1990s, described as 'a generation detached from the solidarity experiences of Timor-Leste's resistance era' (Arnold 2009:380). It is said that retribution for past wrongs can be carried across four generations within Timorese society, with members having responsibility to uphold the honour of their families in feuds with others. In Timor-Leste, hostilities between families were fuelled by Indonesian recruitment of Timorese youth to *ninja* and *gadapaksi* groups to attack pro-independence groups. Thus Timorese social divisions have a long history. Historic patterns of group conflict have been part of Timor-Leste's cultural and political landscape dating back to the Portuguese era but the majority of groups formed during the Indonesian occupation (Scambary 2013). Experiences in other post-conflict states indicate such groups re-emerge and remobilise at critical junctures of political and social change. In post-conflict South Africa, a study showed that endemic urban violence and crime that had been seen as a product of poverty and marginalisation was principally a result of historic rivalries (Kynoch 2005).

Analysis of the formation of groups and gangs in Timor-Leste has found that of some 300 groups and social movements in the post-conflict period these are:

> predominantly male, span a wide range of ages and often transcend ethnolinguistic boundaries. Their hybrid nature and often overlapping memberships with other groups makes categorisation both difficult and

---

40   Interview, Director, Dili Institute of Technology, 6 September 2005.

contentious … Rooted in East Timorese cultural traditions and history, rather than being fringe elements alienated from society, they play an integral role within their communities as a means of voicing the demands, aspirations and identity of community members. (Scambary 2013)

These groups are complex and adaptable; they may fade with time and/or reshape their identities. They are a major source of engagement for Timorese male youth born after 1990. Many of these youth have been disengaged from the formal economy and national life since they left school.

Table 2 (p. 90) attempts to map these organisations, drawn principally from Ostergaard's Youth Social Analysis and Scambary's research on youth groups and gangs (Ostergaard 2005; Scambary 2006; Scambary 2013) as well as my own research. Youth groups described in chapter two that transitioned into NGOs and CBOs in the post-independence period can no longer be considered youth groups although their members may consider themselves youth leaders. In 2006 the depth of schism between different groups in the community was shocking, but what was not so obvious was that the elements of 'discontentment' changed over the succeeding two years. Distinct phases in the crisis evolved from the clashes between the security forces, to protracted street brawls between ethnically based groups, and finally to conflicts between former clandestine cells and martial arts groups.

During the 2006 crisis, according to a church youth worker, the clear identities of martial arts groups became conflated with east-west rivalries and political allegiances.[41] Rivalry between martial arts organisations led to numerous incidents of violent conflict particularly in the latter part of the crisis. They have been an important source of social engagement for male youth since the Indonesian occupation with a membership strongly linked to the resistance (Scambary 2006). There are 15–20 different martial arts groups, some linked to the resistance movement and others established since independence. The membership of these groups is 20,000 registered and up to 90,000 when including unregistered members. Most are male and between 15–25 years, although the leadership is generally older (Ostergaard 2005; Scambary 2007; Scambary 2011). Young women comprised about 5 percent of the group membership. These groups offer not only physical training to the youth but a needed measure of sociality. They are accused though of promoting rivalry. Their leaders have been criticised for failing to provide a positive orientation or good leadership.[42]

---

41 Interview, Catholic Youth worker, Dili, 15 August 2006.
42 Interview, Coordinator District Youth Council, Suai 4 August 2006.

Table 2: Major Groups Engaging Youth in Timor-Leste

Key: G75 – 1975 generation; GF – Gerasaun Foun; GM – Gerasaun Mileniu (youth)

Type of Group	Leadership	Membership	Activity
Disaffected groups & informal security groups	G75 ex-veterans, GF ex-F-FDTL and police officers, with anti-government grievances	May be aligned with kinship networks or political networks. High participation of unemployed GF and GM.	Anti-government demonstrations, informal security provided incl. summary justice for retribution.
Martial arts (MA) groups	GF – many founded during Indonesian occupation	GM membership of male youth from 15 years old. 5% female participation.	Martial arts training. Group solidarity has led to violence towards other MA groups.
'Kakolok' mystical groups	G75 former clandestine leaders, identified by symbolic scars on their arms.	Mostly 16–35 (GF-GM) male members.	Use potions to draw on power from the ancestors. Were engaged in violence in 2006
Local youth groups	GM male & female bairro or village based.	Bairro/ village GM youth (male and female) with leadership within group.	Involved in music, sports and social service. Some Dili groups became engaged in crime in 2006.
National Youth Council and its affiliates	Secretary of State for Youth and Sport support for youth activities.	District based youth organisations, often GF leaders, GM members.	Sports, music and training for district youth group members.
Church youth groups and Scouts	Catholic church youth leaders, priests, scout leaders.	GM male and female. These are the major source of social activity for young women.	Sports, music and leadership training for youth. Boys tend to drop out at puberty for martial arts membership.
Other civil society groups (NGOs, CBOs)	GF former members of the clandestine student movement who still identify as 'youth'. Above average education.	Issue based, not youth organisations but recognised as such by Ostergaard's typology in 2005.	Community development programs, drawing on donor funds.

The two largest martial arts groups, PSHT[43] and KORK,[44] are rivals who have been blamed for much violence. Both groups claimed to promote national unity and maintained that there are rules to abide by and that violence occurs because the members break the rules.[45] Conflict was generally blamed on the 'code' of defending 'brothers' in the group, often related to personal or family issues, rather than intrinsic differences between the groups.[46] 'Brotherhood' is translated into support for any member who has problems, according to a young female member, who was attracted to her martial arts group for the friendship bonds and sense of belonging.[47] The National Police detective chief estimated that at least twelve East Timorese had been killed and more than 200 injured in the previous two years as a result of fighting among rival *pencak silat* clubs (an Indonesian form of martial arts).[48] Prime Minister Gusmão tried to encourage these groups to operate peacefully, but the continuing deaths of martial arts group members led to these organisations being banned in July 2013.

Violent masculinities in Timor-Leste have been described as enactments that have the aim of reassuring the male himself and 'his' side while simultaneously intimidating the 'other' side into submission (Myrttinen 2005). Largely male international armed forces and UN uniformed police in large numbers further masculinised the social environment. The 'political crisis' of 2006 was dominated by armed conflict and expressions of violent masculinity, with women as notably absent from street violence and public displays of anger (Niner 2011)

Alfredo Reinado, commander of the F-FDTL military police, became an important symbol of violent masculinity. Reinado, together with seventeen of his men and four members of the police Rapid Intervention Unit (UIR), deserted their posts in April 2006 in opposition to the deployment of the F-FDTL against civilians. A westerner from Aileu, Reinado became a hero for young people, particularly the Mambai speaking westerners. Reinado

---

43 *Persaudaraan Setia Hati Terate* (PSHT – often shortened to SH): Lotus Faithful Heart Brotherhood.
44 *Klibur Oan Rai Klaren*, or the Association of People from the Centre (formed in Ainaro, where Mount Ramelau is perceived as the centre of Timor-Leste).
45 Interviews with Provincial leader of KORK, Suai, 6 August 2006 and Provincial leader of PSHT, Suai, 6 August 2006.
46 KORK male member interview, Suai, 6 August 2006.
47 PSHT female member interview, Suai, 6 August, 2006.
48 www.news.com.au/world/east-timor-bans-local-martial-art-pencak-silat-amid-violence/story-fndir2ev-1226725619347

opened fire on F-FDTL, killing a number of men,[49] and evaded the Timorese authorities and Australian forces over the ensuing months. Many youths started to dress like him (Niner 2008). They were fugitives in the hills until Reinado was shot dead at the house of President Ramos Horta on 11 February 2008, an event that marked the end of the crisis after two years of conflict.

Parallels have been drawn with Boaventura's many heroic escapes from the heavy hand of Portuguese authorities in earlier times, due to the limited reach or influence of the Portuguese in the mountain rugged areas (Sengstock 2008). Many believed that he had been endowed with the spirit of the 'warrior king' *Dom Boaventura*.[50] Reinado was thus elevated into a cult figure, symbolising the heroic rebel fighting against an unjust state.

Civil Society Peace Building Activism

In 2006, all development agencies and NGOs turned their attention to responding to the humanitarian crisis, and tertiary educational establishments in Dili were closed for much of the year. While the new generation of school leavers became embroiled in the violence, the 'young generation' activists of the clandestine struggles were leading a peace campaign. The year 2006 was in some ways a defining moment for civil society, which engaged actively in peace-building activities. Activities to promote national unity were immediately organised by the NGO Forum, the umbrella organisation for Timorese civil society organisations. It set up a National Unity Committee to organise a public information campaign, set up reconciliation programs in the burgeoning camps of internally displaced people (IDPs) and monitor the emergency distribution program implemented by international agencies in the IDP camps. During the ethnic tensions, civil society activists from east and west worked together

---

49 This clash was not foreseen but was captured on film (Personal communication with SBS reporter David O'Shea, Hotel Dili, August 2006). Details on http://news.sbs. com.au/dateline/four_days_in_dili_130664.

50 Reinado had only spent a few years of his childhood within the Timorese community. His traumatic childhood experiences at the hands of the Indonesian military have been described elsewhere (Niner 2008). Reinado sought to strengthen his credentials with the cultural power of Dom Boaventura, the *liurai* of Manufahi region, who united several kingdoms to participate in the last major uprising against the Portuguese in 1912. A ritual ceremony, presided over by Manufahi elders in 2007, reportedly endowed Reinado with the late Boaventura's supernatural powers, shortly before he escaped an assault by the Australian International Stabilisation Force on his hideout in Same, capital of Manufahi district.

to promote peace and reconciliation. Banners were raised across the capital with slogans such as *'Ema Ida, Nasaun Ida'* ('One people, one Nation'), appealing for people to see themselves as one nation (Wigglesworth 2013a).

Large amounts of money were allocated to peace-building activities by the Timorese government and international agencies, but Timorese NGOs had difficulty in getting support for their activities. For instance NGOs had been promised funds by the government for their peace activities the funds failed to arrive, forcing activists to go into debt to complete the activity[51] and exacting a response: 'The government wants to centralise the peace process. They are not interested in the NGO contribution to peace'.[52]

Timorese activists were concerned that short-term solutions were being put in place, some of which benefited only certain people and therefore had the potential to further divide the community. For instance all IDPs received rice handouts but families that remained in their houses received nothing even though they were perhaps just as needy.[53] Local NGOs wished to develop ongoing and sustainable programs working in the communities, but they felt that most money was being allocated to handouts and large consultations without follow up and ongoing support.[54]

Internally displaced people (IDP) camps had been set up for the escalating numbers of IDPs, reaching 150,000 in mid-2006. Management committees were appointed for each camp, coordinated by INGO representatives. Some international NGOs started to implement emergency projects directly in the IDP camps rather than enlist the support of their local NGO partners.[55] No emergency funding was available to local NGOs; rather they were contracted to work under the INGOs. Activists were angry at this apparent return to a marginalised role for Timorese NGOs. As one expressed:

> after the crisis the local organisations did not get much opportunity to be involved directly to prevent further violence and help the victims in terms of access to resources. It was a repeat of 1999–2000, in terms of distribution it was under INGOs. In spite of their increased experience by 2006, local NGOs were only permitted to work as subcontractors under the INGO's name.[56]

---

51   Personal communication, Lemos, Melbourne, 30 May 2008.
52   Personal communication, Magno, Melbourne, 2 November 2007.
53   Personal communication, Lemos, Melbourne, 30 May 2008.
54   Personal communication, Reis, Melbourne, 26 October 2007.
55   Personal communication, Reis, Melbourne, 26 October 2007.
56   Interview, Lemos, Dili, 11 August 2006.

Many IDP camps were still operating two years after the start of the crisis. This renewed 'emergency' funding enabled INGOs to set up peace building and conflict resolution programs in communities where they had not previously worked. These, it was claimed, often ran parallel to existing programs of local NGOs.

The security situation, moreover, made it impossible for many local NGOs to continue their development programs, so regular NGO activities were brought to a halt, either because staff were directly affected by the crisis or because the movement of people disrupted communities. Some were told that their grants were being suspended because normal program work could not proceed, leaving Timorese managers with an obligation to pay their staff but without funds to do so.[57] INGO power over funding forced local NGOs to submit to donor demands making it difficult for local organisations to make any decision for themselves. Timorese activists thus felt unsupported both by the RDTL government and international donors that were doing little to support the NGOs' own initiatives.

Timorese activists did play a significant part in the promotion of traditional forms of mediation during the 2006 crisis, which gained considerable credibility in conflict resolution efforts. *Nahe biti* (spreading the mat) ceremony depends on the judgements of the *lian nain* and the council of elders made up of male members of local elites. Elders sit together and discuss problems before coming to a common decision about the outcome (Trinidade and Bryant 2007). *Nahe biti* is 'an evolving process that ultimately seeks to achieve a stable social order within society' (Babo-Soares 2004). Thus a Timorese path was established that uses alternative models which harmonise with the traditional life of the people. Traditional processes are respected by the community, thus overcoming the legitimacy problems of elected representatives. Josh Trindade proposed a solution to the 2006 crisis which involved the traditional practice of *juramento* (binding oath) at national level and the construction of *uma lulik* (sacred houses) at national and district levels. In this, Trindade was proposing not only the use of traditional Timorese belief systems at community level, but also that Timorese political leaders should be brought into the process to resolve political conflicts at the topmost level of government.[58]

---

57 Interview, Lemos, Dili, 11 August 2006.
58 Email from Josh Trindade sent 17/10/06 as an open letter to the Prime Minister and to the East Timorese people, entitled 'An oath for the People of Timor: Strengthening unity, ending violence and cherishing culture through customary Timorese belief structures'. The proposal was not taken forward.

Many independence activists played a key role in the formation of new civil society organisations in after the Indonesians left. Jose Magno was a founder of the KSI which works in research and conflict management. Like ETSSC activists Natalino Gusmão Soares and Antero Bendito da Silva, he is now a lecturer at the National University.

Civil society has also promoted sustainable development using the customary practice of *tara bandu*, a Timorese resource management system.[59] Environmental NGOs such as *Fundasaun Haburas* work with local communities to impose ritual prohibitions on the use of natural resources to protect the environment from activities which exploit natural resources or threaten endangered plant and animal life and has been described as

59   Interview, Haburas staff, Dili, 4 October 2005.

'traditional ecological wisdom'.[60] While this collaboration of NGOs with customary leaders and practices had started long before the crisis, national and international organisations started to recognise the value of these processes for conflict resolution and restoration of harmony.

Summary

Development in Timor-Leste was severely derailed by the political crisis which broke out in 2006 and continued into 2008. Its causes were complex, and actors many, fuelled by underlying resentment about the lack of improvement in the lives of the majority of the population living in poverty. The existence of historic rivalries between communities gave rise to the renewed leadership for settling old scores using the foot soldiers of unemployed and frustrated young men. Many youth blamed their leaders for the violence that they themselves perpetrated, including payback for past wrongs in inter-family feuds, that were a response to hierarchal power structures of groups and gangs in which youth operated. The reverence for Alfredo Reinado demonstrates that youth can be uncritical of strong, violent, masculine figureheads such as those that have been revered through Timorese history. Kinship relations and powerful leadership figures have been shown to have a strong influence on the actions Timorese youth, and while discourses about youth tended to see them as a 'problem' and the provision of formal work as a solution, the drivers of discontent were and are more complex.

Youth of the 'millennium generation' have gravitated to groups which offer them a sense of place, uncritically accepting leadership from kinship or patronage networks. Meanwhile the *Gerasaun Foun* activists have provided leadership to draw on 'traditional' local cultural practices to make peacebuilding and development interventions more relevant to local communities while promoting principles of equality and sustainability.

---

60   Demitrio do Amaral de Carvalho, founder and Director of *Haburas*, the first and only environmental NGO in Timor-Leste, winner of the Goldman prize 2006 (www. goldmanprize.org/node/95).

Chapter Six

LANGUAGE IDENTITY AND EDUCATION FOR DEVELOPMENT

This chapter describes how language impacted on culture and class identity in independent Timor-Leste. How have different generations of Timorese experienced education? And how have these experiences shaped perceptions of Timorese identity, culture and aspirations for the development of the country?

Generational Perspectives on Timorese Identity and Language

A gap between the Portuguese speaking '1975 generation' leadership and the majority of tertiary-educated Indonesian-speaking Timorese stems from their belief in the superiority of Portuguese education over the Indonesian system. This resulted in the infamous remark by Mari Alkatiri, recounted bitterly by many Timorese activists, that Indonesian qualifications were akin to '*super mie*' (instant noodles that are cheap, poor quality and quick to cook) (Hughes 2011:1508).

The political leadership from the '1975 generation' had internalised the official Portuguese ideology that being civilised (*civilisado*), they were superior to the people they left behind in the villages (Hill 2002:84). Concepts of cultural superiority instilled by the Portuguese education system extend beyond language. In the Timorese diaspora in Australia, Portuguese-educated Timorese reportedly referred to the 'etiquette of Portuguese culture' and looked down on traditional practices such as 'sitting on the floor and eating with fingers. The Portuguese taught them to eat with knives and forks' (Crockford 2007:183). For the Portuguese-educated Timorese, their language was a source of identity that carried prestige and status. Although the majority of their generation did not have access to any formal education, Portuguese was used as the language of the resistance, and the right of children to learn Portuguese was one of the rights that the resistance was fighting for after the Indonesians forcibly closed down Portuguese schools (Hill 2002).

Ordinary rural families had access to education for the first time under the Indonesian regime, so young graduates were often proudly the first educated members of their families. During the Indonesian occupation in 1990 secondary school enrolment was fifty times that during the Portuguese era, and illiteracy rates fell from 90 percent to 52 percent of the population (Cox and Carey 1995:46). By the end of the Indonesian occupation the first-year school enrolment rate, which was almost equal for boys and girls, reached 90 percent (Nicolai 2004:44). Graduates of the Indonesian education system consider themselves as the elite of their generation because of their higher education qualifications, in contrast to the limitations of their illiterate parents. For example Rei recounts his family's experience:

> Being illiterate meant you had no access to another perspective apart from what the colonialist told you. My father saw many examples of the Portuguese manipulating *Maubere* people. Then under the Indonesians, a common tactic was to kill *Maubere* people who had signed a false confession that they could not read. (Rei 2007:58).

The first year of a new Portuguese-Tetun primary school curriculum was taught in 2000 to new school entrants. Each year a new grade started to use the new curriculum as they rose up through the school. Students who had started school in the Indonesian period have continued learning using the Indonesian curriculum. Indonesian speaking graduates replaced large numbers of Indonesian teachers who fled in 1999, although most lacked teaching qualifications.

The experiences of school during the Indonesian occupation for almost all my research participants were marked by disruptions due to the political environment and their roles in the clandestine movement. Students who enrolled in school shortly after Indonesia established schools in 1980–81, and continued their education up to university level, were close to completing their degrees at the University of Timor-Leste in the tumultuous year of 1999 when the Indonesian administration ended. Many did not graduate for many years after. As most students experienced interrupted or incomplete education, both during and after the Indonesian occupation, it is not unusual for adults to still be attending school, or returning to complete their schooling as adults. Since independence, large age ranges in class have been common (World Bank 2003). As much as 70 percent of children do not complete grade nine (now signifying the completion of 'basic education') and it takes 11.2 years on average to graduate from grade six, double the amount of time it should (Shah 2012:31 f/n 2).

From the perspective of young Timorese the value of language is of an altogether different order to that of the older generation. The young tend to see language exclusively as a practical tool. The Indonesian speaking Timorese were forced by their experiences to disconnect emotionally from the Indonesian language and this generation is often unable to accept Portuguese as a desirable language or cultural symbol (Dibley 2004). Dibley asserts that their understanding of language as a practical tool is exemplified by the fact that many Timorese activists express a preference to learn English, because it provides a window to the world, rather than Portuguese, which only opens communication with the small number of Lusophone countries, mostly in distant Africa.[1] As well, the replacement of Indonesian with Portuguese, in the eyes of Indonesian speaking Timorese, is simply replacing the language of one coloniser with another.

While young Timorese say they do not like Portuguese because it is a difficult language, a less mentioned reason for not wanting to learn it stems from the attitudes of some Portuguese speakers. Several young people who claimed to not speak Portuguese admitted that they could understand but did not speak Portuguese simply because they felt they would be looked down on by Portuguese speakers. An activist explained:

> If you speak badly you are laughed at. In English you can make mistakes without a problem – the focus is on understanding. It is the colonial mentality in which somebody would be judged by their standard of Portuguese.[2]

In contrast, as most English speaking visitors to Timor-Leste will know, young Timorese use every opportunity to practice their English even if they speak poorly. The likelihood of being shamed when practicing Portuguese has resulted in a preference to learn English.

The RDTL Constitution of 2002 declared Portuguese and Tetun co-official languages and declared English and Indonesian as working languages. The government made a commitment to develop and value Tetun as well as the vernacular languages. The choice of Portuguese as the

---

1   Lusophone countries are Portugal, Brazil (the largest), Mozambique, Angola, Guinea Bissau, Sao Tome and Cabo Verde. In Asia, Portuguese is only spoken in Timor-Leste and Macau, a Portuguese enclave in China.
2   Interview, Austcare national staff, Dili, 25 March 2006.

official language of Timor-Leste was made at the first CNRT[3] conference in Perniche, Portugal in 1998 and was restated at the CNRT Congress in 2000. The decision was not well received by the younger Indonesian educated generation. The inclusion of Tetun as an official language was made a year later as a result of intense lobbying by two younger members of the Constituent Assembly, representing a generation which felt alienated by the adoption of Portuguese as the official language (Leach 2003). The implementation of the Portuguese language policy was made possible by Portuguese Cooperation which financed the development of Portuguese language curriculum and teacher training.

While most Timorese speak Tetun few adults have ever learnt to write it as the majority became literate in the Indonesian language. The use of Portuguese as the language of administration makes them feel like 'outsiders'.[4] This sense of marginalisation amongst the literate population represents a lost opportunity for the new nation, as well as making Timorese identity a question of debate and dissent. While the younger generation consider Portuguese a colonial language, for Timorese leaders it is part of their culture and identity, as indicated by Jose Ramos Horta: 'It was a strategic decision to strengthen the uniqueness of East Timor, the national identity of East Timor' (Ramos Horta 2002).

According to Horta, due to the common ethnic and linguistic roots with the people of West Timor, Timorese leaders were keen to define the unique identity of the East Timorese. They stressed the Portuguese heritage in order to distinguish themselves from the people of West Timor, part of Indonesia. For this generation the decision to reinstate Portuguese as official language was the fulfilment of a long held aspiration.

Tetun was popularised as a national language through its use in Catholic Church mass during the occupation, after the speaking of Portuguese was banned. As noted earlier, Catholicism became popular during the occupation because the Catholic Church was the only institution in the country that supported the human rights of the Timorese. Many people turned to the Catholic Church for protection against atrocities and threats by the Indonesian military. While just a third of the population were Catholic at

---

3   *Conselho Nacional de Resistencia Timorese* – the National Council of Timorese Resistance created as an umbrella to unite FRETILIN and UDT in the lead up to independence. At this meeting the *Magna Carta* was drawn up which outlined the principles on which an independent state of Timor-Leste would be based. The same acronym is used for a new political party created by Xanana Gusmão in 2006–7, indicated as CNRT party in this book.
4   Interview, Lemos, Dili, 11 August 2006.

the end of the Portuguese colonial period, by the end of the occupation 98 percent of people identified as Catholic[5] (Ministry of Health 2003). As a result Catholicism, like Tetun, became a symbol of Timorese identity for most of the population.

The younger generation of Timorese conceived of national identity in ways which contested the official view that Portuguese is part of the identity and culture of the Timorese (Leach 2003). A survey of 320 young people on language, heritage and national identity undertaken in 2002 found that the ability of people to speak Tetun was considered 'very important' by 83 percent of the respondents, but the ability to speak Portuguese was seen as 'very important' by only 24 percent. It also found being born in Timor-Leste or a citizen of Timor-Leste (90 percent of respondents) and being Catholic (81 percent) were 'very important'. This survey was repeated, by Michael Leach, five years later in 2007. The importance of language in relation to national identity for young people was shown to have increased for Tetun from 83 percent to 88.5 percent, but had doubled for Portuguese from 24 percent to 52 percent (Leach 2008). This indicates a growing acceptance of, or resignation to, the Portuguese language policy, but a continuing adherence to Tetun as a unifying language.

Aspects of national identity which find resonance amongst the older and younger generations alike are the Tetun language, Catholicism and the history of struggle of the Timorese against the Portuguese and Indonesian occupiers. According to Ramos Horta, the term *Maubere* was the single most successful political tool of the independence campaign as a symbol of identity, pride and belonging, and the resistance movement was recognised in the Timorese Constitution as a symbol of national identity (Leach 2003).[6]

The Languages of Education

The Constitution acknowledges that Timor-Leste is a multilingual society (Taylor-Leech 2005). However the government did not implement a bi-lingual policy in the early years of independence and the Tetun language, although an official language and widely understood, is not used in most official policy documentation. Thus most of the population, including political leaders and parliamentarians, have a limited grasp of Timor-Leste's laws and policies.

---

5   In the Indonesian census, Timorese had to choose between one of five major religions and almost all chose Catholic.

6   'RDTL *acknowledges and values the secular resistance of the Maubere people against foreign domination and the contribution of all those who fought for national independence*' (RDTL 2002).

The view of Tetun, as insufficiently evolved for use as a national language, can be traced back to FRETILIN's policy statements in 1974 (Hill 2002:78). Ramos Horta (2002) referred to Tetun as a 'rudimentary language' still in need of development, while the Director of the National Institute of Linguistics, responsible for developing Tetun orthography, argued in 2005 that it would take at least ten years for Tetun to be evolved sufficiently for use as the medium of education and administration.[7] The importance of developing the language does not appear to hold a high priority for government. An activist involved in a joint Tetun education project with the Ministry of Education in 2004 experienced Ministry staff looking down on Tetun. Their low opinion of Tetun as a language of education was matched by the lack of any budget for Tetun teaching in the curriculum.[8] Several tertiary-level teachers have observed that opinions prevail within the Ministry of Education that the use of Tetun would result in a 'dumbing down' of the standard of education.[9] This view has inhibited the promotion of a bi-lingual policy. Research has shown that Portuguese in schools is used primarily for presenting teaching material while Tetun is used for explanatory talk (Quinn 2011:272). Tetun then, although an official language, is treated as a poor relation to the 'superior' Portuguese language. Yet the opinion amongst both teachers and students is that English is the 'true international language' while Tetun is widely regarded as the 'true national language' (Molnar 2010:91–92).

The Fourth Constitutional Government designated the first nine years as compulsory primary education, encouraging students to stay in school longer. Timor-Leste's plan for Education and Training commits to Education for All (EFA) and MDG goals on formal and informal education (Ministry of Education and Culture 2006).[10] The EFA[11] global commitment is to ensure that all girls and boys complete a full course of primary schooling

---

7   Personal communication with Director of the National Institute of Linguistics, 1 October 2005. That ten years has no passed but Portugese remains predominant.

8   Interview Timor Aid staff, Melbourne, 7 April 2007.

9   This was mentioned by a DIT language teacher, Dili, 12 August 2006, and by the Director of the Teachers' Training College, Baucau, 18 August 2006.

10   The Government of RDTL has incorporated the provisions of the Constitution and international covenants and agreements such as the Convention on the Rights of the Child (CRC), Millennium Development Goals (MDGs), and Education For All (EFA) as 'a guiding principle in the formulation and implementation of educational policies'.

11   At a meeting of the World Education Forum in Dakar in April 2000 the EFA initiative was adopted. It was subsequently launched by the Food and Agricultural Organisation (FAO) and the United Nations Educational, Scientific and Cultural Organisation (UNESCO) in 2002.

and to eliminate gender disparity in primary and secondary education by 2015.

After independence, the rate of literacy rose, particularly for girls. By the time the 2010 census was undertaken, girls between the ages of 15–19 years had a mean of 7.5 years of education and 86 percent literacy rate, almost equal to that of boys. Literacy rates were 68 percent for all women and 78 percent for all men with literacy levels lower with age for both sexes (NDS 2010).

From a practical perspective at Timor-Leste's independence, just one in twenty people spoke Portuguese while more than four in five spoke Tetun (Ministry of Education and Culture 2006:33).[12] The capacity to implement national policy and programs in Portuguese language was highly constrained by the inability to recruit primary school teachers with proficiency in Portuguese (Nicolai 2004). With the assistance of Portuguese Cooperation, the government implemented compulsory intensive Portuguese language training for teachers and civil servants. Indonesian-educated primary school teachers were intensively trained in Portuguese, but most had no opportunity to use their Portuguese skills within their communities and never spoke Portuguese outside the classroom.[13] The language policy resulted in Portuguese training for teachers becoming the major focus of education policy, even though many other aspects of curriculum development needed urgent attention. Youth literacy in Portuguese has risen from 26 percent amongst 25–29 year olds to 43 percent amongst 15–19 year olds, but three quarters of both age groups are literate in Tetun (Curtain 2012:40).

Although Indonesian continued to be used as a language of instruction, it was no longer taught as a language subject. The standards of Indonesian language started to deteriorate to the point that students were arriving at university without competence in the language of most tertiary teaching.[14] The Ministry of Education and Culture also reported that students are expected to write their theses in Indonesian when they are 'all but illiterate' in the language (Ministry of Education and Culture 2006). It was recognised that the failure to develop language proficiency risked low educational

---

12   Tetun is widely spoken in Timor-Leste. It is a language based on Tetun Terik, spoken in the south and west of Timor-Leste, but incorporating much Portuguese vocabulary. Known as 'Tetun praca' or market Tetun, it became a creolised trading language under colonial rule.

13   I met with a teacher in Baucau in 2008 who learned Portuguese as part of the teacher training program. She said she had not, until our conversation, ever actually spoken Portuguese outside of her school.

14   Personal communication, Magno, Melbourne, 2 November 2007.

outcomes for the primary school graduates who were no longer proficient in the Indonesian language but faced moving into secondary education where teachers were largely proficient 'only in teaching in the Indonesian language and continue to use textbooks in this language'. Effective training for proficiency in teaching in Portuguese in their subject specialisation was called for to avoid 'undue deterioration on the quality of instruction and student learning' (Ministry of Education and Culture 2006:25). Youth literacy in Indonesian is on the decline, but the 50 percent literacy rate is still higher than for Portuguese amongst 15–19 year olds.

Once the Indonesians left, many activists looked for ways to contribute to national development. Alberto, Egy and Simão are activists from Suai who worked together in the ETSSC up until 1999. Some became involved in teaching in the secondary school due to the shortage of trained teachers when then Indonesian teachers fled in 1999, but they also continued their civil society work.

Secondary high schools started receiving Portuguese educated primary graduates before the new curriculum was available. In 2009, teachers in Suai described having to interpret their Indonesian curriculum texts into Tetun to be able to teach, as students lacked Indonesian proficiency and teachers lacked Portuguese.[15] In mid-2008, all the secondary schools were closed for

---

15   Personal communication, Vicente and Barreto, Suai, 28 August 2009.

three months to provide intensive Portuguese language training to teachers. Such attention was not given to Tetun, to assist teachers to learn the official Tetun orthography. Indeed, between 2004–7 schools were told to prioritise the teaching of Portuguese over Tetun because of the latter language's 'tentative status' (Shah 2012:35).

The unequal implementation of the official language policy with respect to the two official languages has disadvantaged young Tetun-speaking Timorese. Some school children, who started their education during the Indonesian occupation, did not have Tetun classes in school. For instance a 19 year old girl in Suai who had attended one year of post-independence primary school and four years of junior high and secondary school had never received any tuition in the official Tetun orthography.[1] Further, two university students in 2012 revealed that they saw 'official Tetun' as a different language from the Tetun they speak daily. They are learning the official orthography at university, but their lack of confidence in it is evident from their expressed preference to write Tetun as it would be spoken.[2]

Now the language issue has refocussed on maternal languages. Language has been found to be the main factor contributing to school dropout, grade repetition and low enrolment rates in the Timorese education system, according to the Advisor on Maternal Languages in the Ministry of Education.[3] A new language of instruction policy has been drafted and passed through the parliament which promotes mother tongue instruction as the focus of early years schooling and reprioritises Tetun as a viable and important national language (Shah 2012:37). The policy, based on international best practice, aims to assist young learners to transition to learning in the official languages.

Language Policy Effects on Social and Economic Participation

One of the impacts of the language policy was that it curtailed hopes of many tertiary educated graduates for getting a job in government.[4] Government officials argued that the process of recruitment for a government job is open

---

1   Interview female member of PSHT, Suai 6 August 2006.
2   Personal communication with two university students, Bairro Pite, August 2012.
3   Agustinho Caet, Advisor on Maternal Languages, Ministry of Education, Email to the ETAN list Re: UN Special Rapporteur Report - Mother Tongue Education Recommended for Timor-Leste, 23 June 2012.
4   As a result, many have sought work in the NGO sector, which, apart from work as school teachers, is the major source of paid employment outside of Dili.

to any of the three languages, Portuguese, Indonesian and Tetun, but in practice applicants described facing interview questions in Portuguese which they could not understand.[5] Although some observers pointed to the fact that non-Portuguese speakers did in fact work within the government, the lack of language proficiency was widely believed by young people to be the major constraint to entering the labour market (Ostergaard 2005:18). Activists expressed their anger at government officials using Portuguese while knowing that few people understood it:

'If someone tries to speak Portuguese with me I am unhappy – I feel they are looking down at me. The older generation occupied government. Even if we have good knowledge we cannot get a position. They marginalised the young generation'.[6]

Carey suggests that the generation schooled during the occupation felt that their educational experience was being 'set at naught' and feared the new Portuguese educated generation would leap-frog them, taking on key political and administrative posts as the 1975 elite moved on, so the Indonesian educated generation could well become a 'lost' generation (Carey 2003).

Tetun is replacing Indonesian for documentation within the NGO sector, although Timorese NGO staff as well as journalists generally had no opportunity to learn to write Tetun in the official orthography. Yet journalists have been unfairly criticised by the leadership for their poor standard of Tetun and failure to use official Tetun.[7]

While official documentation is produced exclusively in Portuguese, the umbrella organisation of NGOs, FONGTIL, is critical that Timorese civil society is denied the opportunity to contribute to national policy development. Even a law concerning the registration of NGOs, passed by the Ministry of Justice in 2006, was provided to the NGOs in Portuguese in spite of the fact few NGO staff can understand the language, and resulted in multiple unofficial translations being produced. Even the Ministry staff did not understand it correctly, giving different interpretations to visiting NGOs.[8] This demonstrates the importance of Tetun being used as an equal official language.

5   Interview, Gusmão Soares, Dili, 29 July 2006.
6   Interview, Vicente, Suai, 7 August 2006. This anger referred to was mentioned by the Director of FONGTIL as well as Suai and Dili activists.
7   Criticism, for example, by Director, National Institute of Linguistics, 1 October 2005.
8   Meeting at the Ministry of Justice on behalf of FONGTIL, 2 March 2006.

The majority of Timorese lawyers have achieved their educational qualifications in Indonesian universities, but laws and judicial institutions which provide skills training and licensing of lawyers give preference to Portuguese speakers (Marriott 2011). In 2006 all the Timorese judges failed their competency tests in the Portuguese language and the courts had to continue sitting with foreign judges (mostly Portuguese or Brazilian).[9] Ten years after independence, national laws were still only produced in the Portuguese language, requiring translators to be involved in most trial preparation and court processes. Consequently, the justice system was described as 'highly overburdened and severely dysfunctional' (Brady and Timberman 2006). Blockages in the court system result from the fact that police, lawyers and defendants cannot understand penal codes, statutes and other legal instruments written in Portuguese and testimony have to be translated from other languages. In 2006 the Catholic Commission for Justice and Peace reported that there had been 1,000 rape cases pending since 2000 and not one of them had been solved.[10] By early 2009 there were an estimated 5,000 court cases waiting to be heard.[11] This systemic dysfunction is in no small part due to the language policy, and has resulted in the perception that the national justice system is unsuitable to contribute to resolution of community conflicts.

In 2012 the NGO Fundasaun Mahein (FM)[12] issued a press release expressing concern about the issue of language negatively affecting the development and implementation of Timor-Leste's legal framework. Noting 'a very small minority most notably the country's elite' speak Portuguese, FM pointed out that the government continued to disclose information and produce advertisements for public information in Portuguese. Legislation is not translated into Tetun. As a result, FM suggests that the Portuguese-speaking elite have a 'stranglehold' on the running of affairs in Timor-Leste because civil servants face difficulties working with documents in Portuguese, a language they are not fluent in. Further, 'many within the PNTL and F-FDTL do not understand their organic laws and other

---

9   Personal communication with a Brazilian lawyer, Dili, August 2006.
10   Interview Catholic Commission for Justice and Peace, 25 August 2006. By late 2008 there were six national judges and one foreign judge.
11   Talk by Fernanda Borges, MP, leader of the *Partido Unidade Nacional* (PUN), VLGA, Melbourne, 6 March 2009.
12   Fundasaun Mahein was formed in 2009 in response to the security crisis in 2006, to monitor the security sector. It aims 'to assist in increasing the legitimacy and capacity of the Timorese security sector through citizen participation in the development of relevant legislation, policies and procedures' http://fundasaunmahein.wordpress.com/deklarasaun-misaun/ website accessed 22/7/2012.

relevant legislation and this causes quite some trouble when it comes to their implementation.'[13]

Many educated Timorese, including Members of Parliament, the justice sector, the education sector and civil society, have not been able to participate as effectively in national programs as they could have if the language used was one in which they were competent. National development has thus not taken full advantage of the skills of its educated citizenry.

Education for Rural Development

The vast majority of Timorese families are farming families living in rural areas. Education is not just valued for its own sake, but for how it assists people to make improvements in their lives (SSYS & UNICEF 2005). Access to education has been articulated as a priority for the majority of the population in every district (RDTL 2006), but Timor-Leste's ability to deliver an effective education for the rural majority has been limited by the adoption of a language which is little understood or spoken in rural areas.

Where education is divorced from the reality of daily life, it is common for parents to believe that the education is 'wasted'. When a student's prior knowledge of traditions and practices is not brought into the classroom, a learner will compartmentalise new knowledge, rather than integrate the new with prior knowledge. Students' inability to utilise their new knowledge in their existing world is referred to as 'cognitive apartheid' (Cleghorn 2005:108). An example is a youth in the Lautem district who studied at Fuiloro Catholic agricultural school where he learned animal husbandry, including feed, medicines and breeding. He explained he could not use the skills he learnt because his family does not have the land area and equipment that exists at the school.[14] The young man argued that animals are free to find their own food in Timor-Leste and to keep them like they are kept in Fuiloro, expensive food and medicine would need to be bought. The animal husbandry taught was evidently not adequately adapted to the circumstances of the students.

Even Timorese graduates in agriculture, who might be expected to become agricultural officers or extension workers, have been shown to be ill equipped to support the traditional agricultural systems that are widely used by Timorese farmers. UNTL's agricultural degree is disconnected from an understanding of the local environment, resources or farming systems in

---

13   Fundasaun Mahein Press release 'Access to Security Information and Language Policy in Timor-Leste' email to ETAN list 21 June 2012.

14   Interview, Verupupuk staff, Los Palos, 28 September 2005.

Timor-Leste so the curriculum does not enable students to use their newly acquired knowledge (Janes, da Costa et al. 2003).

Building on the experience of FRETILIN's literacy program and establishment of literacy schools in the liberated areas soon after the occupation, *Dai Popular*, a 'popular education' network of NGOs in Timor-Leste, was formed to promote Freirean principles (Durnan 2005). Popular education is based on the concept that the starting point of learning for change is the existing knowledge of the participants and their environment, a principle that has since been extensively used not only in progressive education but also in development theory and practice. The belief that simple transfer of knowledge does not facilitate true learning was pioneered by Paulo Freire, a Brazilian educator in the 1970s who believed that conventional schooling instilled passivity in students, which he termed 'banking education' (Freire 1972). Freirean educationalists believe that an education system that gives answers but does not encourage questions results in the 'castration of curiosity'. Two key educational principles are that knowledge needs curiosity and that teachers cannot teach without learning at the same time (Freire and Faundez 1989:35). The 'banking education' structures promote the legitimacy of the 'wisdom' of the dominant groups, while the alternative wisdoms of oppressed groups are unrecognised (Ife 1995:96).

Civil society in Timor-Leste is using a community-orientated approach to introducing new skills and knowledge. Sustainable agriculture, centred on organic, family based production, is promoted by over thirty organisations that are members of the HASITIL NGO network. One is PERMATIL, which set out to challenge the normative view that agriculture is undesirable for school leavers by making agriculture more acceptable to young people. Using permaculture methodology, which builds upon traditional composting techniques but also introduces new ideas in land conservation and planting techniques, PERMATIL founder Ego Lemos found a way of involving young people in agriculture by blending art, music and permaculture:

> Young people were not interested in agriculture. Once they had some education they assume agriculture is not a good source of employment. Mostly older people, women and men, would join the groups, so I started a new approach – not only to introduce agricultural techniques. I also used music to introduce agriculture to young people to combine art and agriculture.[15]

---

15   Interview Lemos, Dili, 11 August 2006.

An activist since attending the student rally at Santa Cruz in 1991, Ego Lemos became involved in the Scout movement where he first learned about agriculture. He enrolled in agriculture at university, and later met a permaculture volunteer who arrived in Dili in 1999. He became an international student to obtain a Diploma in Permaculture and formed the NGO PERMATIL to promote permaculture in Timor-Leste in 2002. Ego is also well known as a musician and has performed in Australia and Europe, and uses music in his work to promote agriculture amongst youth.

Image credit: Sam Karanikos Photography

To attract young men and women into agriculture, his permaculture sessions combined socialisation and enjoyment by playing music at the start and end of work sessions. This acted as a bridge to the culture of young people to engage them in work. It was not a fixed program but adapted to the preferences of the community: 'In some areas youth join the older group, in some areas they form separate group for youth, depending what is appropriate for them. A lot are young women,' explained Lemos. By engaging young people in local activities it is less likely they will leave the area and will contribute to rural development.

Subsistence agriculture provides food production for the majority of the population but it is of little interest to economists because of its limited contribution to the market economy. The Timor-Leste Strategic Development Plan 2011–2030 proposes that subsistence farming be *replaced* by smallholder agriculture by 2030 (RDTL 2011:202) in a model of development aimed at increasing marketed production.

Local customary values are intricately tied up with the agricultural system, leading a Timorese researcher to describe it as 'subsistence culture'.[16] To replace traditional agriculture will not involve just changes in agricultural technique but changes in social and cultural resource allocation. These aspects are unlikely to be adequately addressed by the promoters of modern farming associated with the Green Revolution (RDTL 2011:121). Critics argue that a Green Revolution focus on high input methods in irrigated and high-potential rain-fed areas has marginalised villages that lack access to sufficient water and has led to growing inequalities in Asia.[17] Timor-Leste plans for rice production to become self-sufficient by 2020, but the crop is largely limited to the fertile valleys of four districts (Viqueque, Baucau, Bobonaro and Manatuto) and involves just 23 percent of the population (UNDP 2006). Maize production involves 60 percent of the population but the majority of Timorese households cultivate it in areas with a slope of over 26 percent (RDTL 2011:118). Thus most families will be unable to engage in 'green revolution' methods of intensive agriculture. Skills to enhance traditional agriculture, to make it more productive and marketable, are much needed, and for this the younger generation needs to receive an education that enables them to make improvements in local productivity and storage of food. If their means of subsistence is 'replaced' rather than their farming capacities enhanced and developed, the more vulnerable Timorese living in the rural communities will be further marginalised.

Summary

Timorese identity is seen differently by each generation in accordance with their particular historic experience and, associated with that experience, their access to education. Although Tetun is overwhelmingly recognised as

---

16   A term used by Abel dos Santos, Director of Community Development, UNTL, on field work in August 2013.

17   http://www.ifpri.org/sites/default/files/pubs/pubs/ib/ib11.pdf

the principle language of Timor-Leste, it has been regarded as inferior by Portuguese speakers and not promoted as an equal national language.

This has resulted in an education and administrative system that appears foreign to the majority of Timorese and irrelevant to their daily lives. The teaching in the Portuguese language has contributed to poor educational outcomes because it is not well understood or used in most Timorese communities. Learning is known to be most effective where it builds on the existing knowledge of the participants and their environment. If education is seen to hold value only for life outside the rural communities, its impact will be the outflow of youth to the towns where these people can look for work opportunities and an urban lifestyle. To improve food production and reduce poor nutrition, youth need to be educated so they have the skills and motivation to establish family businesses in food production and or processes or marketing of local products. Young people have to be promoted as change agents in strategies that could assist their families to overcome poverty and hunger in the countryside.

Chapter Seven

PARTICIPATION IN GOVERNANCE AND LOCAL DEVELOPMENT

Every citizen has the right to participate in development that affects them. This chapter reviews how the Timorese have participated in and benefited from the development processes taking place in their country. Since the country was embroiled in crisis from 2006 to 2008, stability returned and new services have been provided, such as pensions for veterans and their widows, made possible by a changed economic environment, as oil royalties came on line to support the national budget. Nevertheless members of the population have little access to decision making structures and the stark poverty in rural areas is largely unchanged. Effective structures for the broader participation of the population, to enable them to hear and be heard by the government, are yet to be established. Civil society, an alternative channel for engaging the people in development, has grown and been influenced by a dozen years of international agency engagement in development in Timor-Leste, but now faces new challenges.

'We had to make policies to buy peace'

After the Gusmão government took office in 2007, it took a high spending approach to resolve the problems of the country. Benefitting from the sub-stantial oil revenues which began flowing in 2005, the initial 2008 national budget plan of $347.8 million jumped to $773.3 million to resolve social problems created by the crisis. More than 10,300 IDP families received a one-off cash payment of up to US$4,500 for house reconstruction to achieve the closure of dozens of IDP camps holding a total of approximately 100,000 IDPs.[1] There were also cash payouts for the 600 'petitioners' dismissed from the F-FDTL in 2006. The impact of the 2008 global price

---

1   Ministry of Social Solidarity - Press Release, 26th November 2008. *Hamutuk Hari'i Futuru* program 'together we build the future'.

hikes for rice and fuel on vulnerable groups required subsidies to be provided, and, according to Prime Minister Gusmão 'We had to make policies to buy peace'.[2]

Of great importance to the rural economy has been the provision of pensions. In 2008 a pension scheme for over 60 year olds was introduced, providing $20 a month for each of these people, distributed through the Suco Council. The provision of age pensions has brought increased cash into the communities and benefited whole families. For instance it is said that some families are better able to meet their cash needs such as paying school fees for their grandchildren, but it also places a huge demand on the national budget.[3]

The government's election promise of national electrification required capital withdrawals from the Petroleum Fund in 2012. In 2013 the total annual budget was $1.8 billion, largely financed by withdrawals from the Petroleum Fund in 2013 ($1.2 billion) and unexpended funds previously withdrawn in 2012. Assets in the Petroleum Fund totalled US$11.777 billion at the end of 2012. Suai has been isolated from the nation's capital for the past ten years due to the poor roads described at the start of this book. It is now the focus of a major government development plan, the South Coast Project, that will include building a port and logistics base in Suai (Covalima District), a refinery and petrochemical plant in Betano (Manufahi District) and a liquified natural gas (LNG) plant in Beaço in Viqueque District, connected by a six lane highway along the south coast. These grandiose plans are in spite of the fact that the road quality from Dili to Suai and Viqueque remains a key obstacle to producers living in these remote south coast districts. Poor roads have also been identified as a major impediment to delivering a better health service.[4]

Health is one of the more impressive areas of improvement in the past ten years, with the under-five infant mortality rate almost halving to 55 per 1000 in 2010, from 104 in 2000.[5] Life expectancy overall has risen to 62 years, but this, coupled with the high fertility rate of 6.2 (up from 5.3 in 1990), contributes to a high population growth rate (3.2 percent), which could lead to doubling the population in seventeen years (RDTL 2011:109).

---

2   Lindsay Murdoch, 'Timor Collides with its future', *The Age*, Melbourne 22 November 2008.

3   Personal communication, Barros, Suai, October 2011.

4   Seminar presentation by Dr Nelson Martins, Minister of Health at Victoria University, 8 November 2007.

5   UNICEF www.unicef.org/infobycountry/Timorleste_statistics.html, accessed 15 April 2013.

The maternal mortality rate remains one of the highest in the world, with 42 percent of deaths of females aged 15–49 being related to pregnancy.

The UNDP Human Development Report of 2013 indicates the country has raised its Human Development Index (HDI) value to 0.576 (from 0.418 in 2000), ranking 134 out of 187 countries and rising into the medium human development category, up from low human development in 2009. But there are inequalities across the population (UNDP 2013). Of great concern is the rate of malnutrition, now affecting 58 percent of children under five, which led the United Nations Special Rapporteur on Extreme Poverty and Human Rights, who visited Timor-Leste in November 2011, to state:

> A harsh reality of entrenched poverty and rising inequality hides behind rapid macroeconomic growth indicators. Recent economic growth has not translated into sustained improvements in living conditions or job creation for the great majority of Timorese people ... Poverty remains pervasive and widespread with 41 percent of the population living on less than one dollar a day. Fifty-eight percent of Timorese children suffer from chronic malnutrition (Carmona 2012).[6]

Poverty is a major cause of malnutrition, often a product of a family's inability to produce or buy adequate food. A mother's level of education, knowledge and ability to make decisions within the family are important indicators of family health. The Rapporteur welcomed an increase in budget allocations for social services in 2012 but was 'concerned by the fact that the budget allocation to physical infrastructure is disproportionately high at the expense of desperately needed health services and quality education provision. Investing in health and education is an investment in the future of Timor-Leste and is critical for sustainable people-centred development' (Carmona 2012). Local economic development is unlikely to keep pace with population growth, so poverty can be expected to increase. This leads Harris and O'Neil to believe there is still a risk of future instability (Harris and O'Neil 2011:233).

Equality of Participation in Local Governance

The concept of decentralisation has been on the agenda since independence but it has not advanced significantly. Rather, a strong central control since

---

6   www.ohchr.org/Documents/Issues/Poverty/StatementSRPovertyTimorLeste_en.pdf

independence has left little role for decision making at District and sub-district levels. In 2003, the FRETILIN government (2002–2006) commissioned a Local Government Options Study to consider the process of decentralisation and alternative models for local governance. The government proposed Sub-District level municipalities within five regions, with representative offices of the Ministries planned for implementation in 2007 (Ministry of State Administration 2003). A change in government after the political crisis in 2006 led to a reassessment of the chosen option for municipalities. The fourth constitutional government favoured the existing district boundaries, even though some argue these boundaries do not offer sub-districts adequate road access to the district centre for service delivery.[7] Legislative delays resulted in the establishment of local municipal decision making being postponed to 2013–14, and then further delayed to 2017.

The first Suco council elections took place in 2005, opening new forms of participation through Suco level governance structures in 442 local 'Suco' councils, including specific roles for women and young people. These built upon the experience of the Community Empowerment Program (CEP), embracing both traditional and modern ideas of political legitimacy, which included designated seats for women and young people. In this way the Suco Council co-opted existing local authority structures balanced by modernising elections (Cummins 2011). The *Conselho Suco* (Suco Council) includes the Suco Chief (*Chefe Suco*), the chiefs of each hamlet (*Chefe Aldeias*), two women, a male and female youth (defined as between 17 and 30 years old) and an elder (defined as over 60 years). This structure aimed to blend the traditional leadership of older males with democratic expression involving women and youth (formerly without voice) in local governance structures.

When the first national Timorese elections for the *Suco* and *Aldeia* council representatives took place in September 2005, the concept of local elections based along party lines was a foreign creation and was considered divisive. The electoral process has been viewed with some discomfort in the communities where 'a clash of paradigms' with local values exists (Hohe 2002). The *Chefe de Suco* was in the past considered a representative of the entire community, but after the multi-party elections, the elected *Chefe de Suco* was regarded by many people as representing only those that voted for him or her, so many *Chefes* could no longer mobilise the whole community but only their supporters.[8] Timorese researchers have found that a Suco

---

7   Interview, Borges, Dili, 4 October 2011.
8   Personal Communication, Martins, Dili, 15 August 2006.

chief who is independent of political parties is more likely to work directly to improve people's lives, as he is not beholden to his party (dos Santos and da Silva 2012:211). In contrast to consensus-based decision making that prevails in traditional government, competitive democracy is seen to create distrust, reduce cooperation and create conflict which can lead to violence (Gusmao 2012:183; Magno and Coa 2012:169). The historical experience of conflict between political parties sometimes brought negative memories but more often the political parties were blamed directly for creating conflict from the top level down where 'people are unable to disentangle political violence from party politics in their village' (dos Santos and da Silva 2012:211–213). The perception that Timorese political leaders act in their own interests or that of their party rather than in the interests of the community has reduced cooperation and increased conflict between members of different parties within the Suco (Gusmao 2012:183; Magno and Coa 2012:171). It also resulted in accusations of nepotism and graft being linked to the concept of 'democracy', as also happened in the first 'democratic' elections in Mozambique when Mozambicans observed political leaders corruptly acquiring resources to strengthen their own positions.[9] There, many people protected their interests by withdrawing engagement with the state rather than exerting voice through participation and advocacy (Lubkemann 2001). In Timor-Leste the party system of democracy is seen by many in the rural areas as less appropriate than the customary system which strives for harmony.

There are several sources of legitimacy for leadership, such as membership of a *liurai* house (Cummins and Leach 2012:98) or involvement in resistance struggle (Gusmao 2012:184). In 2005 a young woman named Lucia Guterres was elected as *Chefe de Suco* at just 25 years of age from a field of five candidates in remote Fatululik *Suco* in Covalima district. It was reported that her active leadership in the clandestine youth movement since the age of 16 generated support.[10] This is an indication of how active and committed women and young people can be, given leadership opportunities once they have proven their abilities.

The Community Leadership Law defines the role of the Suco council as 'to organize the community's participation in the solving of its problems, to uphold its interests and to represent it whenever required' (Law 3/2009, article 2.1). The Suco Councils are expected to engage in consultation and

---

9   I was resident in Pemba, Mozambique, at the time of the first democratic elections in 1993 and heard these comments during work in the rural communities.

10   A film was made about Lucia's life by a student film maker from Melbourne University, entitled *Lucia*.

discussion with the whole community for planning and execution of community development activities, resolution of disputes and establishment of prevention mechanisms and protection for domestic violence victims. The Law designates the Suco Chief as responsible for most Council functions and gives the Suco Council responsibility for 'assisting' and 'advising' the Suco leader (Asia Foundation 2009).

The Suco Councils, which are not a formal part of government, report to the government appointed Sub-District Administrator who reports to the District Administrator. As there has been no decentralisation of power to the District Administration, the locally elected representatives at Suco level have had limited roles in local development decision making. Village level infrastructural projects (such as community centres, schools, clinics, water and irrigation projects) can be presented by the Suco council for funding by the Local Development Program (LDP) operated by the Ministry of State Administration and Territorial Management (MSATM). The Local Development Program (LDP) supports only community infrastructure projects; thus many new construction companies established themselves to bid for the construction projects on offer.

Following a pilot project for budget decentralisation in two sub-districts, the LDP was extended to eight districts with a budget of US$3.50 per head of population in 2009 for projects proposed by Suco Councils.[11] The District Assembly, consisting of Suco Council representatives and District and sub-District officers as non-voting members, could allocate 30 percent, with the remaining 70 percent allocated for Suco infrastructural projects by prioritising and approving projects.[12] Once funded, approved contractors bid to implement the work. The country is thus still in early stages of developing structures and mechanisms for devolved forms of governance. Although many civil society organisations are relatively well established and experienced, these were not included as potential partners to government programs at community level.

Women are involved in local governance in two ways. A total of ten women were elected as Suco Chiefs in 2009, while all Suco councils have women representatives. In a research project into women in local councils in 2011, four women Suco Chiefs were interviewed.[13] These chiefs believed

---

11   The Ministry of State Administration and Territorial Management Press Release, 2 February 2009.

12   Interview MSATM staff, 22 September 2011.

13   I undertook 'the inclusion of women in decision making' research project in October 2011 on behalf of the International Institute for Democracy and Electoral Assistance

their election was due to having a good level of education or for their prior leadership in community activities. Membership of Liurai families was also known to be a factor in at least four of the total of ten women Suco Chiefs. Women Suco Chiefs were said to be inclusive in leadership practices, promoting community consultations and involving other council members.

The Suco women representatives, on the other hand, sometimes struggled to play their role. Some explained that male Suco Chiefs carried out their business with minimal discussion with other Suco Councillors. A common complaint was that male Suco Chiefs often did not pass on information to the council members, or that the women would not be invited to training activities for Suco Council members. One key issue was that the Suco Chief gives leadership in customary governance processes from which women members are barred. A male Suco Chief described the Suco Council as having horizontal and vertical elements, the horizontal being the core group of the Suco Chief and Aldeia Chiefs, and women and youth representatives were seen as vertical elements with lower importance in decision making (Wigglesworth 2013b).

The 'old institutional figures' are concurrently leaders of both the traditional and modern spheres, whereas the 'new institutional figures' of women and youth are limited to exercising their leadership through the modern sphere (Cummins 2011). That women's representatives are not valued as equal members of the Suco Council is also corroborated by Timorese researchers who reported that people viewed the roles of some elected Suco council members as limited because 'the government has not involved them directly as representatives of the people' (dos Santos and da Silva 2012:209, 215). Different understandings and expectations about the role of the women Suco representatives resulted from the existence of parallel but not integrated customary and national governance systems. In one Suco it was noted the Suco Chief always attended training activities with the male youth representative known as the Assistant Suco Chief, or 'secretary' (Wigglesworth 2013b). Secretarial duties are often given to the male youth representative because men can be privy to customary laws as well as Council aspects of decision making. Thus their assistance is of more value to a male Chief than a woman in the same role (Cummins 2011).

Domestic violence is a major social issue in Timor-Leste. A Law Against Domestic Violence (LADV) was passed, in 2010, which defined all domestic

---

(IDEA). My thanks to IDEA in Sweden for permitting my use of the research for further publication.

violence (DV) as a criminal offence and made it mandatory to pursue cases of DV once they are reported. The law recognises DV as physical violence against the person as well as sexual, psychological and economic violence through threats, coercion, use of force, manipulation, insult and damage to personal items. It upholds the right to live without violence and provides support and assistance to victims of DV through government services including a specialised police unit, women's shelters and health services (SEPI 2010).

Domestic violence is considered a crime, but interpretations allow for different ideas of legitimacy within communities and government. The traditional systems view DV as a minor justice issue to be dealt with customarily (dos Santos and da Silva 2012:218). Such cases are typically brought before the *lia-nain* and the *Chefe Aldeia*, and may be taken to the *Chefe Suco* for resolution before being referred to the police if a mutual agreement is not made within customary justice processes. The woman would be represented by male members of her family. In cases of sexual assault the victim receives no recompense, but a payment may be made to her father (Mearns 2002:39–40). A woman representative on a Suco council complained she was not permitted to play a role in the customary process or raise issues in relation to it at the Suco meeting. She believed that she should have been able to participate in the process to support women's rights (Wigglesworth 2013b). A crime against a woman, such as domestic violence or rape, is not considered a violation of the individual, but a transgression of the social order seen to threaten the peaceful living together of members of a community. As the practice of *barlake* binds the two families together, the woman may be compelled to live in a vicious cycle of domestic violence because it is impossible for her family and relatives to give back to the husband's family the goods donated at the wedding (Silva 2011 159). As a result of this and in spite of the law, all but the most severe cases continue to be dealt with through customary justice.

It appears the meaning of domestic violence is being redefined so that community justice processes are not perceived as breaking the law. Villagers have been found to ascribe a meaning to the term '*violencia domestica*' that excludes what is considered 'normal' violence, described in Tetun as '*violencia iha uma laran*' (violence in the home).[14] It is suggested that some cases of DV would be locally judged to be 'civil', or outside the DV law, rather than

---

14 Comments made during research on Attitudes and Perceptions of young men and women on gender and masculinities in Timor-Leste, commissioned by Paz y Desarrollo (PyD) in 2013. Thanks to PyD for permission to use this material.

'criminal' because it is dealt with by *lisan*. Thus the mode of justice defined the severity of the case rather than the other way around (Cummins 2010:155). By redefining DV, community leaders were trying to reconcile traditional communal values in customary law with the individualistic values of the LADV, because they said the government has not yet explained to them how to resolve the contradictions.[15]

Many cases of domestic violence that have been taken to the police have been withdrawn on account of women's economic dependence on their husband, threats of violence, and police referring 'minor' cases (where there is no bleeding or obvious injury) back to village officials to be dealt with through traditional justice processes (Nixon 2012). While all cases of DV should be referred to the police, this is not the case, indeed it would be understandable that in some less severe cases a woman would not necessarily want to charge her husband and risk breaking up her marriage. She would, however, want social pressure to be applied that could discourage his violent behaviour.

In contrast, the experience in Mozambique at independence was to replace customary justice processes with 'popular tribunals' comprised of community leaders and 'lay judges' whose function was primarily to mediate between parties 'in accordance with good sense and justice, bearing in mind the principles that guide the building of a socialist state' (Gundersen 1992:257). The majority of cases were family conflicts brought by women, receiving judgements in courts that were 'local, informal and accessible' by community leaders within the principles of the constitution. These popular tribunals would have at least one woman lay judge recruited by the party women's organisation, often representing a rather traditional set of values (Gundersen 1992:278). This experience of modifying customary justice processes showed that social change needs to be negotiated according to local experiences and priorities, but it can be impeded by top down inter-national processes supporting only the implementation of human rights (Corradi 2011:18).

Involving local women is shown to be effective elsewhere also. In Papua New Guinea the Australian government supported a program in which women were appointed as village magistrates in informally held village courts. Ten years ago these were mostly men but, now that women are appointed, local women have the courage to present cases of domestic violence which

---

15   Wigglesworth, A. and dos Santos, A. B. (forthcoming 2016) 'Customary values and global influences in youth attitudes to gender and violence in Timor-Leste', *proceedings of the Timor Leste Studies Association Conference 9–10 July 2015.*

may previously have been unreported.[16] Globally it is found that to redress underlying power imbalances in customary justice, it is women who need to be provided resources and opportunities to shape customary law through their own strategies (Williams 2011:66).

Top Down and Bottom Up Development Aid

Local engagement in development activities by local and international NGOs is another opportunity for peoples' active citizenship. Small scale funding provides the means for initiatives of local actors to be supported and, unlike the LDP infrastructure projects, to build community capacity in a variety of technical areas.

Effective working relationships between international agencies and Timorese activists can support mutual exchange and involvement of local people in the design and implementation of a program. NGO capacity development is required to establish the skills and values needed for an organisation to survive. In consultations with local NGOs it was clear that most of the newer NGOs viewed their ability to obtain funding as a top priority, while more established NGOs had a clear vision and mission and demonstrated commitment to engage meaningfully in community development.[17] To be effective, NGOs must build a constituency with communities and a constructive relationship with government. Without such a basis for ongoing development, NGO community development activities are likely to end when the funding ceases.

Effectiveness of outcomes is highly dependent on partnership arrangements. Community participation in planning and implementation of development programs has become a fundamental principle of good development planning (Fowler 2000). This is because effective development is not achieved by projects operating in parallel to local systems, but through the new and the old finding common ground through working together. This point is highlighted by a Timorese activist who argued that development projects which are designed and implemented in parallel to local structures are unable to touch local understandings and therefore do not bring about change:

---

16   Elizabeth James, 'The female hand of justice', *Focus* Vol 27 No 2 pp.24–25, AusAID June-Sept 2012.
17   Lessons from two of my consultancies: the Evaluation of FONGTIL (Wigglesworth & Soares 2006), and the East Timor Civil Society Strengthening Program (January-February 2008) for the Australian Council of International Development.

> Timor-Leste needs to bring back the tradition and culture of respect for nature and respect for each other. Otherwise we are flying in the air but never landing. We need to revitalise local knowledge not just depend on the outside world.[18]

Culturally appropriate processes can position local people as experts by integrating their knowledge into new learning, but different groups of people (men and women, young and old) may require different strategies to make changes, especially when this might challenge longstanding customs (Harris 2007). Some more mature Timorese NGOs have learnt much from INGOs regarding participatory development methods, but many newer CSOs are said to have no idea about such methods.[19] INGOs can provide new strategies and tools for participatory processes to enable views of different members of the community to be heard rather than rely on the village leaders. Activists need exposure to effective techniques for inclusive community consultation, to overcome the influences of hierarchical approaches that have been part of their lived experiences, while INGOs need an understanding of local culture; thus mutual learning is required. According to one activist meaningful understanding of local culture by international organisations will produce successful activities:

> INGOs can make change but they have to come through the right way. This is based on the way of life of the people. If something is very new it should be introduced through the way of life of the people so it is easy to adapt.[20]

Where development interventions are disconnected from the roots of society, without due consideration for the traditions and culture of the people, the introduced intervention is likely to fail because inclusive participatory processes are critical to effective community development (Mosse 2001; Fowler 2002). During the periods of emergency, and reconstruction periods, many INGOs were in intense competition for humanitarian aid resources available. In Timor-Leste the focus on competitive tendering and budget accountability gave limited opportunity for attention to understanding the cultural and historical context (Wigglesworth 2006). This resulted in models of post-conflict humanitarian responses which were imported and

---

18   Interview, Lemos, Dili, 11 August 2006.
19   Interviews, Former Oxfam Australia staff, 27 March 2007 and Plan Australia staff 20 March 2007.
20   Interview, Vicente, Suai, 7 August 2006.

pre-defined and did not permit local participants to take ownership of project activities.

Since then there has been greater support for local NGOs, but many have struggled to cope due to short contracts, sometimes for just a few months. This mode of operation has resulted in excessive workloads due to constant proposal writing and being required to use multiple different reporting and accountability formats, often in English. It has placed a huge and unfair burden on inexperienced NGO staff to meet donor demands.[21] Some NGOs have struggled with administrative and financial accountability systems to receive continuous donor funding and grow, especially as competent staff are often lured away to better-paid jobs in international organisations.

Building a broader range of skills and capacities within local civil society requires long-term commitment. INGOs that have supported programs with the explicit objective to strengthen the capacity of local NGOs include Irish Concern and Canadian Catholic Organisation for Development and Peace, which have now closed their programs due to their global cost cutting, a loss to Timorese civil society. In other cases, donor power can be compounded by the often stated view that Timorese 'lack capacity', which is so widely expressed by donors that activists frequently refer to their own 'lack of capacity' without defining what they lack capacity to do. Such relationships between donor and local NGO instil a sense of inferiority or inadequacy in a person rather than overcoming capacity limitations. Meanwhile Timorese's respectful attitudes conferring power and authority to the donor are often irrespective of age and experience.

International donors need to control where funds are going and to show results, while Timorese NGO's have to work with the money they receive in relation to external factors rather than what they need (Hughes 2009:128–130). Donors often quickly disburse large amount of funds in a fixed budget time frame, in other cases their policies limit grant giving to a particular sectoral focus. Thus NGOs may apply for activity funding in areas that they lack experience because they cannot get support for the work they most wish to do. Also NGOs may be offered money for community activities but not for staff salaries or office costs. Thus the decision making about programs does not always allow NGOs to set their own priorities; instead local NGOs are forced into a service delivery role (Hunt and Wigglesworth 2013).

---

21   Interview, Plan Australia staff, Melbourne 20 March 2007.

A perceived lack of capacity of local NGOs sometimes results in contracts to deliver parts of programs through an approach that might be described as 'a mechanism to deliver foreign aid, not short-term building blocks of long-term change' (Edwards quoted in Pearce 2000:32). Globally, INGOs have been accused of cutting corners on the principles of effective partnerships, participatory processes including gender equality and active citizenship, due to 'short-termism, control orientation and standardisation that have infected development work for a decade or more'. Edwards argues that the evidence about effective development strategies is clear:

> we already know the principles of project success: engage with local realities, take your time, experiment and learn, reduce vulnerability and risk and always work on social and material development together (Edwards quoted in Pearce 2000:32).

Partnerships between international and local organisations enable mutual exchange and learning and the knowledge of each partner is valued equally, described by Fowler as an 'authentic partnership', in contrast with the common use of the term 'partnership' in contexts of unequal power relationships between donor and recipient (Fowler 2002). A Timorese researcher describes the existence of two forms of relationship – a contractual one for local NGOs fulfilling a technical service delivery role, and a partnership relationship which supports local NGO's own values and projects (Tchailoro 2013). Local NGOs need to be conscious of the importance of bottom-up development not only in relations with INGOs but also with the communities in which they work.

Anthropologists have analysed development practice not just in relation to those being 'developed' but also in relation to the 'developers' and their projects. It is argued that development entails the simultaneous recognition and negation of difference, because Third World subjects are recognised as different on the one hand whereas, on the other, development is the mechanism through which that difference is to be obliterated (Escobar 1997). This process is described by one researcher who questions the value of the kind of development programming taking place in Timor-Leste:

> The legacy of the *malae*[22] period in which Timor-Leste is still partially embedded, is a local civil society landscape composed of institutions which have been trained to think and act as agents of development and are likely to pursue conventional development goals. The radical, the

---

22   A term used by the Timorese to denote a foreigner.

unconventional, the local, indigenous and individual, are being diluted as Timorese come to realise that 'community empowerment' comes with its own 'tied-aid' rules. Local organisational structures, processes, goals and imaginaries, even organisational identities, are reinventing themselves in the image of international development (McGregor 2007:168).

Timorese activists, however, have made a different distinction, arguing 'development' is where they, as Timorese, are the agents of change. This, they say, is not synonymous with 'projects' funded and implemented by donors. 'Projects' in the minds of some Timorese activists are linked with inequality, where the beneficiaries may be selected groups within the community in a process divorced from local decision making and local knowledge. In these cases, the benefits are not expected to continue beyond the funding period because the project did not correlate with local concepts of needs.

The 'Friendship Cities movement' is a unique solidarity program based on citizen-to-citizen relationships being formed between a group of people in Australia with people in a particular district or sub-district of Timor-Leste. This movement was facilitated by the Victorian Local Government Association and Abel Guterres, now Timorese Ambassador to Australia, to ensure that the destruction and violence against the Timorese such as took place in 1999 could not be repeated. It was sending the message: 'You are not alone, we are with you and walk with you' (Kehi:2005). In Australia, local councils committed themselves to support their Timorese counterparts predominantly through voluntary community committees and local fund-raising, although some also supported a part-time paid staff member. A range of different development activities have been implemented in the districts through this movement. The strength of the Friendship Cities movement is that it has brought meaningful engagement to many Australians and many Timorese. A number of Timorese have identified this form of assistance as offering greater equality in relationships than the traditional donor-recipient relationship. A collaborative approach built on locally identified issues and needs is a hallmark of the friendship relationships.

Another important area of civil society action is advocacy. Ten years into independence, there are a number of Timorese NGOs that have established an effective advocacy niche for themselves. This includes NGOs which act as watch-dogs over government practices, for example, *La'o Hamutuk*[23] which provides analysis of the national budget and critiques of

---

23   *La'o Hamutuk* ('Walk Together') is the East Timor Institute for Reconstruction Monitoring and Analysis.

An activist and member of ETSSC as a university student in Dili, Alberto de Jesus Barros became a translator for the UN after they arrived in 1999 where he started to learn about community development. In 2005 he joined the Covalima Community Centre (CCC) supported by Friends of Suai of the City of Phillip in Melbourne, part of the Australian friendship cities movement which formed to support Timorese development after 1999. Alberto is Director of the CCC which runs training progams for youth in computer technology and English as well as community development activities.

expenditure patterns in relation to the budget and donor funds. Another is *Fundasaun Mahein*, which has done similar advocacy work in relation to the security forces since the 2006 crisis, providing constructive criticism and debate to hold the government accountable. Women's NGOs have also engaged in public advocacy which contributed to the legislation on domestic violence, and they continue to actively work with the Secretary of State for Promotion of Equality for the National Action Plan on Gender Based Violence. Advocacy is facilitated by the RDTL government's Transparency Portal, which follows international best practice in making national budget information available to the public, online.[24]

The sustainable agriculture NGO network, *HASATIL*,[25] with a membership of over thirty NGOs, has been successful in establishing an effective

---

24   http://www.transparency.gov.tl/english.html.
25   *HASATIL – Hadomi Sustentabilidade Agricutura Timor Lorosa'e.*

working relationship with the Ministry of Agriculture (MoA). Consultative meetings have been held between NGOs and the Ministry, in Dili and the districts, facilitating dialogue in which members could challenge the government's support of crop production for export over local farming systems and traditional food production.[26] When compared to other ministries, the MoA have been more prepared to debate and collaborate with civil society.

NGOs have also promoted local community voice in relation to national development proposals. The Timorese NGO *Fundasaun Haburas* intervened in plans for the creation of a National Park in the district of Lautem, working with affected communities to re-establish the people's voice in national and regional politics and planning and to enable 'outside' concepts to be reformulated through traditional resource management processes. The government held a 'consultation', at which officials presented national plans that stressed national benefits but failed to recognise local interests or to make any assessment of the community's land and sea management capacities or practices that existed. Technical and scientific knowledge of university educated government officials was assumed to be superior to local knowledge and customs, in a process that reflected the idea that all relevant knowledge lies with the planners and not with the local people (Palmer and de Carvalho 2008). *Fundasaun Haburas* placed emphasise on the need for Timorese to define and develop programs building on knowledge of traditional customs and progressive understandings of individual and democratic rights.

Fewer international organisations are now operating in Timor-Leste, reducing available donors for NGOs, but the Civil Society Fund is a new source of funding established by the Timorese government. This fund is seen by some NGOs as funding non-controversial projects with NGOs that are not critical of government, with an emphasis on service delivery and Catholic Church infrastructure and programs, rather than support to community development (Hunt and Wigglesworth 2013). Timorese civil society organisations have made a significant contribution to engaging with local cultures and structures in development interventions, but the limited support they have received from the Timorese government and the donor community leaves a question mark over whether civil society will continue to grow strong and prosper.

---

26   Interview Lemos, Dili, 11 August 2006.

Summary

Rural communities have been able to participate in local development both through local level councils and aid funded development projects run by international or local NGOs or UN agencies. Both these forms of engagement have tended to be driven by a top down policy approach which does not necessarily open space to work collaboratively in the design and decision making between the local, national, and international actors.

Development decision making has been heavily concentrated in Dili. Structures set up at the Suco level extended democratic processes into the communities with mixed success as party politics became a new source of division. The Suco elections delivered a significant degree of affirmation of the traditional leaders but there is no formal bridge between national policies and customary practices. Individual leaders have to manage both customary practices and national constitutional obligations of local governance, even though these are sometimes incompatible. Male elders continue to dominate, but not always to the exclusion of views of women and younger members of society. Successful female Suco chiefs claim to have gained respect because they had previously done work that benefited the community.

The relationship between Timorese civil society and international agencies has not always promoted mutual learning or strengthening of civil society capacity. Activists have been critical of Eurocentric attitudes and 'service delivery' approach. This has led to a declining number of NGOs engaged in advocacy. As Timor-Leste's greater national economic self-reliance has resulted in declining interest in Timor-Leste by foreign donors, support for local civil society has reduced. Government support of and collaboration with NGOs is limited. Thus the conditions for civil society growth and impact do not support the vibrancy of civil society that was evident in the early years.

CONCLUSION

Development is not a simple process. There are many stakeholders, each with their own agendas, ideas and beliefs about what constitutes appropriate development. Rapid change has taken place in the last decade in Timor-Leste and the progress made by the new country in many ways is a success story, but this is not so for everyone. Lessons for post-conflict development drawn from this study of Timor-Leste highlight the promotion of positive forces of change through engagement of youth and women, and the important contribution of civil society in representing their interests in policy making and program development.

Development and Generational Change

Around the world, young people are drivers of change, wanting a life different from that of their parents and grandparents. *Gerasaun foun* activists sought to contribute to the nation's development, but they also present a different perspective and analysis of national development from either the older 1975 generation or the younger 'millennium' generation. This generation that lived in the turbulent times of the occupation was, nevertheless, nurtured by the customs and culture of their kin. They were eager to rise above the poverty and illiteracy of their families and many became the first literate members in their families. The education by their occupiers prepared them sufficiently in English to become interpreters after the arrival of the international donor community in 1999.

Their analysis of Timorese development is often more reflective of the general view of rural Timorese than can be heard in the corridors of power. Some Timorese activists have started to integrate customary practices into their development programs, such as conflict resolution and ecological practices that have been handed down from their forefathers. As well many women activists have worked hard to bring greater equality into the lives of women. Educated young people have a great capacity to contribute to community development. In Timor-Leste it is commented that while elders are said to be the roots of the tree, keepers of history, tellers of stories and the dispensers of wisdom, young people are the branches and twigs representing the future (Babo-Soares 2003).

Democracy is a central concept of nation building and it is argued that citizens should be active players such that they have 'the opportunity to participate in their own development within a national framework of basic human rights, including justice and freedom from fear, and equality' (Kabeer 2005). Inclusive and participatory development is recognised as good practice at both national and local levels even though, as shown in preceding chapters, in reality much program implementation does not live up to this ideal. A Timorese academic and former activist described the situation of Timor-Leste as a 'laboratory of democracy'.[1] He observed that the Constitution recognises the existence of traditional rights, but this recognition was not built into national policies. Models of development implemented in Timor-Leste have at times produced policies and strategies that do not take into account the existing government and belief systems that dominate the lives of the majority.

Timor-Leste emerged at a time when international aid agencies had adopted the Paris Agreement and committed to a strategic approach in which donors would work with sovereign governments to define and co-ordinate development aid within a national planning framework. Timorese political leaders who lived in Mozambique during the period of its early independence in the 1980s–90s (as did I) well knew of the dire effects of imposed economic restructuring on the population and resisted some of the proposed strategies of the international agencies. However, the UN-managed state administration and democratic processes, as well as the World Bank's management of the development funds for the country, resulted in many state building decisions being made before independence, in May 2002, with inadequate consultation with recognised Timorese leaders. Policies and structures for the new nation included the creation of national security forces that failed to consider the highly political nature of police and army roles, the consequences of which were seen in 2006.

Local participation enables individuals and groups in society to define and 'own' community development activities. For this, unlike with customary decision making, power needs to be shared so that people whose voices were previously unheard can be recognised: community leaders by national leaders; young people by elders; women by men. Youth and women are key stakeholders in Timor-Leste's development, comprising the vast majority of the adult population, and their views need to inform processes of change.

Cultural norms are continually in a state of flux, adapting as new influences come to bear, so what is considered Timorese culture now might be very different from that at the arrival of the Portuguese five hundred

---

1   Personal communication, Magno, Melbourne, 2 November 2007.

years ago. For example, today young Timorese consider that eating rice is Timorese culture, whereas maize and sweet potato were the staples of their ancestors. From a development perspective, the value of that change needs to be considered: polished rice has lower nutritional value than maize and sweet potato, contributing to malnutrition. Nutritional strategies are required to reframe the preferred eating patterns that have now become seen as 'Timorese culture' so that the process of change is guided in a positive direction. Development is effective where it can enhance and guide processes of change.

Local civil society activists with their understanding of both the culture and contemporary development ideas, are a key resource. But Timorese civil society is struggling from limited support from either international organisations or national government. *Gerasaun foun* activists, who felt marginalised by the Portuguese language policy, have again been disappointed that, as civil society activists, their work has not been given due credit by government. Yet a strong civil society is an essential component of nation building.

Two-tier Development

Timor-Leste is a small but complex country, with a hierarchal social structure and many languages, that has been dissected by two periods of colonial domination and a bitter conflict. The 1999 international response to the situation in East Timor was welcomed by the Timorese, but there was disappointment at the domination of policy making and planning by Western development agencies during the initial intervention. However, the journey of independence was made possible through a collaborative effort between the Timorese government and international agencies, a large number of which continue to operate in Dili. Timor-Leste is in the happy position of possessing financial resources from oil and gas revenues that can support its development. In spite of the evident success of the creation of a viable and democratic country, there have been persistent grumblings of discontent about the foreign domination and concentration of development aid in the capital during its short history.

Although there has been a long and enduring relationship of solidarity between the Timorese and international activists supporting their independence struggle, in 1999 many of the donor community were newcomers who arrived knowing little of the history and social complexities of this society.

The experience of international development in Timor-Leste led one activist to observe that the development provided by the outside world does not touch local understandings of the traditional world. He explained that development projects which are designed and implemented in parallel to local structures are disconnected from the roots of society. Projects from the outside world, 'flying in the air but never landing',[2] do not touch the reality of Timorese tradition and culture and are thus unable to bring about fundamental change. The Western models of development in Timor-Leste have at times resulted in a lack of connection between the lived experiences of the majority of rural Timorese and the processes of development being planned and implemented by the government and international agencies.

Timor-Leste has a high rate of adoption of international human rights conventions and with international support has built implementation strategies into plans to achieve the Millennium Development Goals. The rapid change and increasing prosperity in Dili is, however, in stark contrast to the limited opportunities for participation and slow rate of change in the rural areas. Poor statistics in child malnutrition and maternal mortality continue to be of grave concern.

The newly constructed palatial government buildings in Dili sit in shining contrast to the roads which have been allowed to deteriorate to a point that they are a barrier for most of the population to reach Dili. This gives a sense of Dili being a world apart from the rural communities. This inequality of resource distribution is accompanied by a social and psychological gap in national policy making which has not built bridges to the rural reality. The 'old' world of customary life in the communities is dominant in rural areas, where most of the population live, but also is present in urban areas because respect of the word of the ancestors continues to influence the majority of Timorese for whom customary values are at the heart of Timorese culture. From the perspective of some of the national elite, however, animist practices are regarded as 'barbaric customs' and they question whether ceremonial practices such as *barlake* should be 'part of the imaginings about the nation' (Silva 2011:152,161). The notion of Portuguese culture and language being at the heart of the new nation's identity is meaningful to only a small proportion of Timorese. Much of the population struggle with a sense of marginalisation and linguistic inadequacy in the new nation. The question of what development should look like in Timor-Leste remains a key issue that is far from being resolved in the country.

---

2   Interview, Lemos, Dili, 11 August 2006.

Customary leaders have complained of lack of opportunity for dialogue with national decision makers, and that national leaders and officials arrive in the rural areas, present the national perspective and leave without any meaningful dialogue. There is a perception that parliamentarians and government officials make visits to foreign countries but do not visit the rural areas to explain the decisions they are making or share their experiences and views (Wigglesworth 2013b). These are some of the factors that lead local people to feel that the government does not serve their interests well.[3] Greater communication is needed between national policy-makers and local communities. The implementation of national values will require new skills in consultation and democratic leadership, which is far removed from the traditional patriarchal and hierarchal political-military forms of leadership that have been in place in the past. The decentralisation process which would enable local government bodies to have a greater input into local development strategies has been delayed until 2017. So it could be fifteen years after independence before a local governance mechanism is established for national policy to listen to the concerns of rural communities.

Timor-Leste is a functioning democracy that fights well above its weight in the international arena, demonstrated by the initiative to establish the g7+ for learning from development experiences in fragile states. It is spearheading a demand to the international community that aid should be responsive to national plans, and particularly in post-conflict interventions. Their lessons on donor–government relations may be valuable for other post-conflict nations, but a greater attention to government–people relations will be required to achieve the 2012 government motto 'Goodbye conflict, Welcome development' (IV Constitutional Government 2012).

Inclusive Development

Development must build on what already exists. The Portuguese and Tetum translation of 'development', '*Desenvolvimento*', expresses unwrapping. That is unwrapping of existing capacities for growth and change embracing new ideas from outside, but not replacing the old by the new. Subsistence agriculture cannot be replaced as a result of a policy or a development plan,

---

3   Generous donations of financial aid for international disasters approved by the Council of Ministers have been criticised by Timorese activists who argue that more resources should be allocated to overcoming poverty (ETAN posting, 6 February 2014, and ensuing commentary).

but there need to be alternatives available so that people can make choices and their livelihood activities can evolve towards greater productivity.

The inclusion of women and youth in the Suco councils reflects post-independence values of equality and inclusion. Their roles are not equal because customary governance continues to dominate community decision making. The Customary Governance law places the chief as decision makers, and women Suco representatives report that their opinions are not sought. The Suco chief implements both national policy and customary justice but the first level of decision making is customary governance where a typical chief does not consider women have a role. The consequences are particularly stark in relation to domestic violence cases. In customary governance, the abused woman will be represented by males in her family and the LADV is brought into effect only if this process does not bring a resolution. The process needs to be one that ensures the best interest of the abused woman, but neither customary nor national processes currently ensure this because the two systems are not formally integrated.

National systems and policies promulgated by the government have been criticised by community leaders as 'globalisation' because they do not reflect the values of Timorese culture and are seen as contradictory to Timorese customary values (Wigglesworth, Niner et al. 2015). As noted earlier, Timorese cultural values are based on social harmony, in contrast to Western values based on individual rights. To bring local practices in line with Timor-Leste's human rights obligations this difference in world view must be reconciled by active engagement with existing practices.

In the districts, activists pointed out that the dissemination of the LADV took place without any prior dissemination of what gender equality means. Research shows that youth may say they agree with the new principles of gender equality (because they know it is law) but they continue to replicate patriarchal values in their intimate relationships.[4] A real understanding of the underlying principles behind of these policies is needed and this needs to start in school.

There is much evidence globally that women's empowerment and gender equality dramatically enhances the health and well-being of families, reduces child mortality and reduces the incidence of girls being kept out of school (UN 2005). An important achievement in Timor-Leste has been equal rates of enrolment in primary school between boys and girls. Educating girls, at least in primary school, has been accepted since independence with little

---

4   See papers Wigglesworth and dos Santos (2016) and Wigglesworth, Niner et al (2015).

opposition. For teenage women to continue their education outside their home village is more challenging because many are withdrawn from school at puberty, and married or pregnant girls are not permitted to continue in school. Education is a great driver of change. Educated and urbanised young women anticipate having relationships with partners of their own choice, with or without *barlake*, and working outside the home. Young women who leave for further study overseas reject the idea of being 'exchanged for buffalo' altogether (Wigglesworth 2012). Women activists are concentrated in the capital so it is these young women who have the potential to be promoters of an agenda for gender equality in the rural areas by embracing new national standards and adopting them within the framework of their daily lives.

Young people migrating to the towns have had a significant impact on the urban landscape. Many have just a few years of schooling and are inadequately prepared for the highly competitive and extremely small job market. The attraction of city life is, perhaps, encouraged by an education that does not reflect the reality of students' lived experiences, while expectations of youth for a 'modern life' includes access to mobile phones, television and the internet. While youth set their sights on a small number of office-based job opportunities, their potential contribution cannot be channelled in a positive direction. Schools need to prepare young women and men for the world into which they live, offering knowledge about how to uphold national policy principles and to improve their own household economy. New knowledge of agricultural methods, skills for preservation and transportation of food, diversifying food for better nutrition, and how to establish viable businesses, should also be part of the national curriculum.

Gang culture and unchallenged patriarchal acceptance of violent masculine behaviour need to be challenged, and change managed through the curriculum and community structures to bring community attitudes more in line with national policy, particularly amongst the young. Internet access is now common in rural areas and youth report regularly accessing pornography. This has greater deleterious effect on their gender attitudes than any positive impact of national gender equality policies of which they have little knowledge.[5]

The participants in this research pointed clearly to lessons to be drawn from the international intervention in Timor-Leste: in order to promote

---

5   Wigglesworth, A. and dos Santos, A. B. (forthcoming 2016) 'Customary values and global influences in youth attitudes to gender and violence in Timor-Leste', *proceedings of the Timor Leste Studies Association Conference 9-10 July 2015*.

'development' international agencies must know the history and recognise the diversity of interests within society. Partnerships at all levels must be built with a mutual learning philosophy to be able to implement effective and inclusive development. Members of the society who seek change are most likely to contribute to it, thus young men and women have great potential to bring about a change in ideas within their communities. The government and donors need to support locally determined and culturally sensitive approaches to bring about that change. Personal struggles for change should be supported. The lack of such support has led local activists to challenge how institutions are delivering development. Globally, there is much evidence of the need for inclusive practices for effective development, but development practice has too often failed to live up to this ideal.

This story of a major international humanitarian intervention over more than ten years highlights the need to understand the cultural, social and political context such that technical or management decisions can be made while recognising local drivers of change within communities and organisations. It is evident that young women are starting to seek a future for themselves as leaders and that the voices of young rural women will become louder in the future. The gateway to development is local people striving for change, knowing that they have the right to expect greater equality in their own lives, and that there are pathways to achieve this.

REFERENCES

Aditjondro, G. J. (2000). "Women as Victims vs. Women as Fighters." *Asian Regional Exchange for New Alternatives* 16(1): 126–135.

Aird, S., B. Etraime, et al. (2001). Mozambique – the battle continues for former child soldiers. Washington DC, Youth Advocate Program International.

Alkatiri, M. (2005). *Licoes e Dificuldades das missoes das Nacoes Unidas em Timor Leste.* International Symposium on United Nations Peacekeeping Operations in Post-Conflict Timor-Leste. 27–29 April 2005, Dili, UNMIT.

Alves, M. D. F., L. S. Abrantes, et al. (2003). *Written with Blood.* Dili, Office for Promotion of Equality, Prime Minister's Office.

Anderson, T. (2006). "Timor Leste: The second Australian intervention." *Journal of Australian Political Economy* 58: 62–93.

Ansell, N. (2005). *Children, Youth and Development.* Abingdon, Routledge.

Arenas, A. (1998). "Education and nationalism in East Timor." *Social Justice* 25(2): 131–147.

Arnold, M. B. (2009). "Who is My Friend, Who is My Enemy? Youth and Statebuilding in Timor-Leste." *International Peacekeeping* 16(3): 379–392.

Asia Foundation (2002). Law and Justice in East Timor: A survey of citizen awareness and attitudes regarding law and justice in East Timor. Dili, The Asia Foundation.

Asia Foundation (2009). *Knaar Lideransa Komunitaria.* Dili, Ministry of State Administration and Territorial Affairs.

AusAID (2003). "Youth in the Solomon Islands – a participatory study of issues, needs and priorities." from www.ausaid.gov.au/research/pdf/youth_research_report.pdf.

AusAID (2008). A Balancing Act: Implementation of the Paris Declaration in Timor Leste, Office of Development Effectiveness, AusAID.

Babo-Soares, D. (2003). Branching from the trunk: East Timorese perceptions of nationalism in transition. Canberra, Australian National University.

Babo-Soares, D. (2003). "Building a foundation for an effective civil service in Timor Leste." *Pacific Economic Bulletin* 18(1): 108–114.

Babo-Soares, D. (2004). "Nahe Biti: The philosophy and process of grassroots reconciliation (and justice) in East Timor." *The Asia Pacific Journal of Anthropology* 5(1): 15–33.

Barrig, M. (2007). What is Justice? Indigenous Women in Andean Development Projects. *Women and Gender Equity in Development Theory and Practice: Institutions, Resources and Mobilisation.* J. Jaquette and G. Summerfield. Durham Duke University Press: 107–133.

Belton, S., A. Whittaker, et al. (2009). Maternal Mortality, Unplanned Pregnancy and Unsafe Abortion in Timor Leste: A situational analysis. Dili, Alola Foundation.

Blackburn, S. (2004). *Women and the State in modern Indonesia.* Cambridge, Cambridge University Press.

Boserup, E. (1970). *Women's role in economic development.* St Martin's Press, New York.

Brady, C. and D. Timberman (2006). The Crisis in Timor Leste: Causes, consequences and options for conflict management and mitigation, USAID: 60.

Brennan, F. S. (2004). *The Timor Sea's Oil and Gas: What's fair?* North Sydney, Australian Catholic Social Justice Council.

Brunnstrom, C. (2003). "Another invasion: lessons from international support to East Timorese NGOs." *Development in practice* 13(4): 310–321.

Bugnion C et al. (2000). External review of the humanitarian response to the East Timor Crisis: September 1999 to May 2000. Dili, UNTAET.

Carey, P. (2003). "Third-world colonialism, the Geracao Foun, and the birth of a new nation: Indonesia through East Timorese eyes, 1975–99." *Indonesia* 76: 23–67.

Carey, P. (2007). "East Timor: Sectarian Violence and the challenge of Nation-building." Retrieved 2nd March, 2007, from www.theword.ie/cms/publish/article_5000.shtml.

Carmona, M. S. (2012). Special Rapporteur on Extreme Poverty and Human Rights. *Human Rights Council 20th session.* Geneva, United Nations.

CAVR (2005). Chega! Report of the Commission for Reception, Truth and Reconciliation in Timor Leste, Executive Summary. Dili, Commission for Reception, Truth and Reconciliation (CAVR): 215.

Chapman, R. and L. Kelly (2007). *Why understanding organisational values and relationships is important for assessing aid effectiveness – An NGO perspective.* Doing Evaluation Better Conference, Melbourne.

Chopra, J. (2002). "Building state failure in East Timor." *Development and Change* 33(5): 979–1000.

Cleary, P. (2007). *Shakedown: Australia's grab for Timor oil.* Crow's Nest, Allen & Unwin.

Cleghorn, A. (2005). Language issues in African school settings: Problems and prospects in attaining Education for All. *Issues in African Education: Sociological Perspectives.* A. Abdi and A. Cleghorn. New York, Palgrave Macmillian: 101–122.

Connell, J. L., John (2002). *Urbanisation in the Island Pacific: Towards sustainable development.* London, Routledge.

Cornwall, A. (2003). "Whose Voices? Whose Choices? Reflections on gender and participatory development." *World Development* 31(8): 1325–1342.

Corradi, G. (2011). "Access to Justice in Pemba City: How exporing women's lived realities with plural law uncovers programmatic gaps." *Journal of Legal Pluralism* 64.

Cox, S. and P. Carey (1995). *Generations of Resistance East Timor.* London, Cassell.

Crawley, H. (1998). Living up to the empowerment claim? The potential of PRA. *The Myth of Community – gender issues in participatory development.* I. Guijt and M. K. Shah. London, IT Publications.

Cristalis, I. and C. Scott (2005). *Independent women: the story of women's activism in East Timor.* London, CIIR.

Crockford, F. L. (2007). Contested Belonging: East Timorese Youth in the Diaspora. Canberra, Australian National University.

Cummins, D. (2010). Local Governance in Timor-Leste: the politics of mutual recognition. *School of Social Sciences and International Studies.* Sydney, University of New South Wales. PhD.

Cummins, D. (2011). "The problem of gender quotas: women's represetatives on Timor-Leste's *suku* councils." *Development in Practice* 21(1): 85–95.

Cummins, D. and M. Leach (2012). "Democracy Old and New: Traditional Authority in East Timorese Local Government." *Asian Politics and Policy* 4(1): 89–104.

Curtain, R. (2006). Crisis in Timor Leste: Looking beyond the surface reality for causes and solutions. *State Society and Governance in Melanesia Project Working Paper.* Canberra, Research School for Pacific and Asian Studies, Australian National University. 1: 25.

Curtain, R. (2012). A Census Report on Young People in Timor-Leste in 2010. *2010 Timor-Leste Population and Housing Census Monograph series.* Dili, NSD, UNFPA and UNICEF: 76.

Curtain, R. and B. Taylor (2005). Viewing Young People as assets in the development process: Key findings of a national survey in Timor Leste. Dili.

de Araujo, F. (2000). The CNRT campaign for independence. *Out of the Ashes: the destruction and reconstruction of East Timor*. J. Fox and D. B. Soares. Adelaide, Crawford House: 106–125.

DFAT (2001). *East Timor in Transition 1998–2000: An Australian policy challenge*. Canberra, Department of Foreign Affairs and Trade.

Dibley, T. (2004). Habits of language: The impact of colonial languages on the attitude and experience of the Indonesian speaking Timorese. *Faculty of Arts*. Sydney, University of Sydney: 100.

dos Santos, A. and E. da Silva (2012). "Introduction of a modern democratic system and its impact on societies in East Timorese traditional culture." *Local Global: Identity, Security, Community* 11: 206–220.

Drysdale, J. (2007). Sustainable development or resource cursed? An exploration of Timor-Leste's institutional choices. *Fenner School for Environment and Society*. Canberra, Australian National University.

Durnan, D. J. (2005). Popular Education and Peacebuilding in Timor Leste. Armadale, University of New England: 193.

Durnan, D. J. (2009). *Popular Education & Peacebuilding in Timor-Leste: Theoretical Foundations*. Understanding Timor-Leste, Dili, Swinburne Press.

Edwards, M. (2001). Introduction. *Global Citizen Action*; (ed) M. Edwards and J. Gaventa. London, Earthscan.

Escobar, A. (1997). "Anthropology and development." *International Science Journal* 49(154): 449–599.

ETAN (1999). "East Timor's social justice groups rebuild." *Peace and Environment news*. Retrieved 24/5/2005, from http:/perc.ca/PEN/1999-11/s-etan4.htm.

ETAN (2000). "ETSSC Resource list." Retrieved 6/6/2005, from www.etan.org/et2000a/march/5-11/11etsc.htm.

Eyben, R. and S. Ladbury (2006). Building effective states: taking a citizen's perspective. Brighton DRC Citizenship, Participation and Accountability, IDS.

Fernandes, C. (2008). "The road to INTERFET: Bringing the politics back in." *Security Challenges* 4(3): 83–98.

Fernandes, C. (2011). *The Independence of East Timor: Multi-dimensional perspectives – occupation, resistance and international political activism*. Brighton, Sussex Academic Press.

Figueira-McDonough, J. (2001). *Community Analysis and Praxis: Towards a grounded civil society*. Ann Arbor, Sheridan Books.

Fowler, A. (2000). *The virtuous spiral: a guide to sustainability for NGOs in international development*. London, Earthscan.

Fowler, A. (2002). Beyond partnership: getting real about NGO relationships in the aid system. *NGO Management*. M. Edwards and A. Fowler. London, Earthscan: 241–255.

Freire, P. (1972). *Pedagogy of the Oppressed*, Penguin.

Freire, P. and A. Faundez (1989). *Learning to question: a pedagogy of liberation*. Geneva, WCC Publications.

Freitas, J. C. (2005). "Decentralisation in Timor-Leste: Issues and Challenges." *Development Bulletin* 68: 20–23.

Freitas, S. (1994). The Indonesians teach us how to hate their violence but also how to resist: East Timor 19 years of resistance. *Department of Social and Community Studies*. St Albans, Victoria University: 50.

Gaventa, J. (2004). Towards participatory local governance: Assessing the transformative possibilities. *Participation: from Tyranny to Transformation: Exploring new approaches to participation in development*. S. Hickey and G. Mohan. London, Zed Books: 25–41.

Gaventa, J. (2006). Perspectives on Participation and Citizenship. *Participatory Citizenship; Identity, exclusion, inclusion*. R. Mohanty and R. Tandon. London, Sage Publications: 51–67.

Gaventa, J. and G. Barrett (2012). "Mapping the Outcomes of Citizen Engagement." *World Development* 40(12): 2399–2410.

Grenfell, D. (2007). "Making Modernity in Timor Leste." *Arena Magazine* 90: 9–12.

Grove N et al. (2007). Like Stepping Stones in the river: Youth perspectives on the crisis in Timor Leste. Dili, Plan Timor Leste: 55.

Gunawardena, C. (2002). Youth and education. *Sri Lankan Youth: Challenges and responses*. S. T. Hettige and M. Mayer. Colombo, Friedrich Ebert Stiftung: 89–118.

Gundersen, A. (1992). "Popular Justice in Mozambique: Between State law and Folk law." *Social and Legal Studies* 1(2): 257–282.

Gunn, G. (2003). "Rebuilding agriculture in post-conflict Timor-Leste: A critique of the World Bank role." *Portuguese Studies Review* 11(1): 187–205.

Gusmao, A. (2012). "Electing community leaders: diversity in uniformity." *Local Global: Identity, Security, Community* 11: 180–191.

Gusmao, X. (2000). *Resistir e Vencer – To resist is to win*. S. Niner (ed.). Richmond, Aurora Books.

Hanlon, J. (1986). *Beggar Your Neighbours: Aparteid power in Southern Africa*. London, Catholic Institute for International Relations

Harris, C. (2006). *Muslim Youth – tensions and transitions in Tajikistan*. Boulder, Westview Press.

Harris, C. (2007). Pedagogy for Development: Some reflections on method. *Working Paper 289*, Institute of Development Studies, Sussex University, Brighton: 34.

Harris, V. and A. Goldsmith (2011). *Security, Development and Nation-Building in Timor-Leste*. London and New York, Routledge.

Harris, V. and A. O'Neil (2011). Timor Leste's future(s): Security and stability 2010–20. *Security, Development and Nation-Building in Timor-Leste*. V. Harris and A. Goldsmith. London and New York, Routledge.

Hill, H. (2002). *Stirrings of nationalism in East Timor – Fretilin 1974–1978, the origins, ideologies and strategies of a nationalist movement* Otford, NSW, Otford Press.

Hohe, T. (2002). "Totem polls: Indigenous Concepts and 'Free and Fair' elections in East Timor." *International Peacekeeping* 9(4): 69–88.

Hohe, T. (2003). "Justice without judiciary in East Timor." *Conflict, Security & Development* 3(3): 335–357.

Howell, J. and J. Pearce (2001). *Civil society and development: a critical exploration*. Boulder, Colorado, Lynne Rienner Publishers.

Howley, P. (2005). "Bougainville: a case study of cultural traditions." *Development Bulletin* 67: 61–63.

Hughes, C. (2009). *Dependent Communities: Aid and politics in Cambodia and East Timor*. Ithaca, New York, Cornell University.

Hughes, C. (2011). "The politics of knoledge: ethnicity, capacity and return in post-conflict reconstruction policy." *Review of International Studies* 37(4): 1493–1514.

Hughes, C. (2011). "The politics of knowledge: ethnicity, capacity and return in post-conflict reconstruction policy." *Review of International Studies* 37(4): 1493–1514.

Hunt, J. (2002). Caritas Australia's response to the East Timor crisis: Evaluation Report. Sydney, Caritas Australia.

Hunt, J. (2008). Local NGOs in National Development: the case of East Timor. *Social science and planning, School of Global Studies*. Melbourne, RMIT University: 384.

Hunt, J., A. Bano, et al. (2001). *Making the most of the capacity of local NGOs in relief, reconstruction and development: the case of East Timor.* Rethinking humanitarianism conference, University of Queensland, University of Queensland printery.

Hunt, J. and A. Wigglesworth (2013). 'Civil Society in Transition'. *Understanding Timor-Leste 2.* H. Loney et al. Hawthorn, Swinburne Press: 251–256.

Hurford, C. and M. Wahlstom (2001). OCHA and the Timor crisis 1999: An independent study for OCHA. Dili.

Hynes, M., J. Ward, et al. (2004). "A determination of the prevalence of Gender-based Violence among conflict-affected populations in East Timor." *Disasters* 28(3): 294–321.

Ife, J. (1995). *Community development: Creating community alternatives – vision, analysis and practice* Melbourne, Longman.

International Crisis Group (2006). Resolving Timor Leste's Crisis. *Asia Report No.120.*

International Dialogue on Peacebuilding and Statebuilding (2011). A New Deal for engagement in fragile states. *4th High Level Forum on Aid Effectiveness.* Busan.

Isin, E. and B. Turner (2002). *Handbook of Citizenship studies.* London, Sage Publications.

IV Constitutional Government (2012). 'Goodbye Conflict, Welcome Development' AMP Government Snapshot (2007–2012). Dili.

James, R. (2001). *Power and Partnership? Experiences of NGO capacity building.* Oxford, INTRAC.

Janes, J., H. da Costa, et al., Eds. (2003). *University education for the agricultural development of East Timor.* Agriculture: New Directions for a New Nation – East Timor. ACIAR Proceedings no 113.

Jaquette, J. and K. Staudt (2007). Women, Gender and Development. *Women and Gender Equity in Development Theory and Practice: Institutions, Resources and Mobilization.* J. Jaquette and G. Summerfield. Durham, Duke University Press: 17–52.

Kabeer, N. (1994). *Reversed realities: Gender hierarchies in development thought.* London, Verso.

Kabeer, N. (1999). "Resources, Agency, Achievements: Reflections on the measurement of women's empowerment." *Development and Change* 30: 435–464.

Kabeer, N. (2005). *Inclusive citizenship – Meanings and expressions.* London, Zed Books.

Killick, T. (1998). *Aid and the political economy of policy change.* London, Routledge.

Kinghorn, M., F. Pires, et al. (2005). Engaging Civil Society Project – Final Project Evaluation. Dili, Catholic Relief Services: 34.

Kumar, K. (1998). Postconflict elections and international assistance. *Postconflict elections, democratisation and international assistance.* K. Kumar. Boulder, Lynne Rienner.

Kynoch, G. (2005). "Crime, conflict and politics in transition-era South Africa." *African Affairs* 104(416): 493–514.

La'o Hamutuk (2008). "Timor Leste Petroleum Fund." Retrieved 27/10/2008, from http://www.laohamutuk.org/Oil/PetFund/05PFIndex.htm#PFCC.

Leach, M. (2003). "Privileged Ties: Young people debating language, heritage and national identity in East Timor." *Portuguese Studies Review* 11(1): 137–150.

Leach, M. (2008). "The neglected state-builder: Cuban medical programs in the Pacific." *Arena Magazine* 98.

Leach, M. (2008). "Surveying East Timorese tertiary student attitudes to national identity 2002–2007." *South East Asia Research* 16(3): 405–431.

Lloyd, G. (2000). The diplomacy on East Timor: Indonesia, the United Nations and the international community. *Out of the Ashes: Destruction and reconstruction of East Timor.* J. Fox and D. Babo-Soares. Adelaide, Crawford house: 79–105.

Lubkemann, S. (2001). Rebuilding local capacities in Mozambique: the national health system and civil society. *Patronage or Partnership: Local capacity building in humanitarian crises*. I. Smillie. Bloomfield, Kumarian Press: 77–106.

Mackay, A. (2005). Mainstreaming gender in United Nations Peacekeeping training: examples from East Timor, Ethiopia and Eritrea. *Gender, Conflict and Peacekeeping*. D. Mazurana, A. Raven-Roberts and J. Parpart. Lanham, Rowman & Littlefield Publishers: 265–279.

Magno, J. d. C. and A. Coa (2012). "Finding a new path between *lisan* and democracy at the *suko* level." *Local Global: Identity, Security, Community* 11: 166–178.

Marks, M. (2001). *Young warriors – Youth politics, identity and violence in South Africa*, Witwatersbrand University Press.

Marriott, A. (2011). The legal profession in Timor-Leste's justice sector reconstruction: Opportunities and constraints. *Security, Development and Nation-Building in Timor-Leste: A cross-sectoral assessment*. V. Harris and A. Goldsmith. London and New york, Routledge: 103–124.

Martin, I. (2000). The popular consultation and the United Nations Mission in East Timor *Out of the Ashes: Destruction and reconstruction of East Timor*. J. Fox and D. Babo-Soares. Adelaide, Crawford House: 136–150.

Martinkus, J. (2001). *A dirty little war*. Sydney, Random house.

McGregor, A. (2007). "Development, Foreign Aid and Post-development in Timor Leste." *Third World Quarterly* 28(1): 155–170.

McKay, J. (2004). Reassessing Development Theory: Modernization and beyond. *Key Issues in Development*. D. Kingsbury. Basingstoke, Palgrave: 45–66.

McWilliam, A. (2005). "Houses of Resistance in East Timor: Structuring Sociality in the New Nation." *Anthropological Forum* 15(1): 27–44.

McWilliam, A. (2007). East and West in Timor Leste: Is there an ethnic divide? *The Crisis in Timor-Leste: Understanding the past, imagining the future*. D. Shoesmith. Darwin, Charles Darwin University Press: 37–44.

Mearns, D. (2002). Looking Both Ways: Models for Justice in East Timor, Australian Legal Resources International.

Methven, S. (2006). Strengthening capacity of CSO in local and national development processes for the achievement of MDGs in Timor Leste, UNDP/UNV; End of project evaluation., INTRAC: 27.

Ministry of Education and Culture (2006). Education and Training: Priorities and proposed sectoral investment program, Government of Timor Leste.

Ministry of Health (2003). Timor Leste 2003 Demographic and Health Survey. Dili.

Ministry of State Administration (2003). Local Government Options Study – Final report. Dili.

Molnar, A. K. (2010). *Timor Leste: Politics, history and culture*. London and New York, Routledge.

Morison, M. (2009). *Democratisation and Timor Leste afer UNTAET: Towards participatory intervention*. Understanding Timor Leste, Dili, Swinburne Press.

Moser, C. (1991). Gender Planning in the Third World: Meeting practical and strategic gender needs. *Changing Perceptions: Writings on Gender and Development*. T. Wallace and C. March. Oxford, Oxfam: 158–171.

Mosley, P., J. Harrigan, et al. (1995). *Aid and Power: the World Bank and policy based lending Vol 1, Ch.2*. London, Routledge.

Mosse, D. (2001). 'People's Knowledge", Participation and Patronage: Operations and representations in rural development. *The New Tyranny?* B. Cooke and U. Kothari. London, Zed books: 16–35.

Moxham, B. (2004). "Avoiding indebtedness and underdevelopment: Lessons for Timor Leste." from www.cadt.org/imprimer.php3?id_article=998.

Moxham, B. (2004). "The World Bank in the land of Kiosks: Community Driven Development in East Timor " *Development in practice* 15(3&4): 522–528.

Myrttinen, H. (2005). "Masculinities, Violence and Power in Timor Leste." *Lusotopie* 12(1–2): 233–244.

NDS (2008). Timor Leste: Poverty in a Young Nation. Dili, National Directorate of Statistics, Ministry of Finance.

NDS (2010). Timor Leste Demographic and Health Survey 2009–10. Dili, National Directorate of Statistics, Minisry of Finance.

NDS & UNFPA (2012). Gender Monograph. *2010 Timor-Leste Population and Housing Census Monograph series*. Dili: 111.

Nicholson, D. (2001). The Lorikeet warriors – East Timorese new generation national resistance 1989–99, Melbourne University.

Nicolai, S. (2004). *Learning independence: Education in emergency and transition in Timor-Leste since 1999*. Paris, UNESCO.

Niner, S. (2008). "Major Alfredo Alves Reinado: Cycles of torture, pain, violence." *Austral Policy Forum*. Retrieved 16/5/08, from www.globalcollab.org/nautilus/australia/apsnet/policy/policy-forum/2008/niner-reinado.

Niner, S. (2009). *Xanana Leader of the struggle for independent Timor-Leste*. North Melbourne, Australian Scholarly Publishing.

Niner, S. (2011). "Hakat Klot, Narrow Steps." *GeoJournal* 13(3): 413–435.

Nixon, R. (2012). *Justice and Governance in East Timor: Indigenous approaches and the 'New Subsistence State'*. London and New York, Routledge.

Nussbaum, M. (2000). *Women and Human Development: The Capabilities Approach*. Cambridge, Cambridge University Press.

OECD (2006). Promoting Pro-Poor Growth: Key policy messages, Organisation for Economic Cooperation and Development

Ospina, S. and T. Hohe (2002). Traditional power structures and local governance in East Timor – a case study of the Community Empowerment Program. Geneva, Graduate Institute of Development Studies.

Ostergaard, L. (1992). *Gender and Development: a practical guide*. London, Routledge.

Ostergaard, L. (2005). Timor Leste Youth Social Analysis Dili, World Bank: 59.

Palmer, L. and D. d. A. de Carvalho (2008). "Nation building and resource management: the politics of 'nature' in Timor Leste." *Geoforum* 39: 1321–1332.

Parpart, J. (1995). Post-modernism, Gender and Development. *Power of Development*. J. Crush. London, Routledge: 253–265.

Patrick, I. (2001). "East Timor emerging from conflict – the role of local NGOs and international assistance." *Disasters* 25(1): 48–66.

Peake, G. (2013). *Beloved Land: Stories, struggles and secrets from Timor-Leste*. Melbourne, Scribe.

Pearce, J. (2000). Development, NGOs and civil society: the daebate and its future. *Development, NGOs and Civil Society*. D. Eade. Oxford, Oxfam GB.

Philpott, S. (2006). "East Timor's double life: smells like Westphalian spirit." *Third World Quarterly* 27(1): 135–159.

Pinto, C. (2001). The student movement and the independence struggle in East Timor: An interview. *Bitter flowers, sweet flowers: East Timor, Indonesia and the world community*. R. Tanter, M. Selden and S. R. Shalom. Sydney, Pluto press Australia: 31–41.

Pinto, C. and M. Jardine (1997). *East Timor's Unfinished Struggle: Inside the Timorese Resistance*. Boston, South End Press.

Planning Commission (2002). National Development Plan. Dili.

Preece, J. and D. Mosweunyane (2003). *Perceptions of citizenship responsibility amongst Botswana youth*. Gaborone, Lightbooks.

Quinn, M. (2011). *The impact of policy on language and learning:the experience of teachers*. New research on Timor Leste, Dili, Swinburne Press.

Ramos Horta, J. (1987). *Funu: The unfinished saga of East Timor*. Trenton N.J., Red Sea Press.

Ramos Horta, J. (2002). "Talking point forum." Retrieved 26/3, 2007, from http://news.bbc.co.uk/1/hi/talking_point/forum/2026934.stm#4.

RDTL (2006). Combating poverty as a national cause: Promoting balanced development and poverty reduction. Dili.

RDTL (2011). Timor-Leste Strategic Development Plan 2011–2030. Dili.

Rees, E. (2003). "The UN's failure to integrate Falinil veterans may cause East Timor to fail." *Onlineopinion*. Retrieved 13/02/, 2007, from http://www.onlineopinion.com.au/view.asp?article=666.

Regan, A. (2005). "Clever people solving difficult problems: perspectives on weakness of the state and the nation in PNG." *Development Bulletin* 67: 6–12.

Rei, N. (2007). *Resistance: A childhood fighting for East Timor*. Brisbane, University of Queensland Press.

Remenyi, J. (2004). What is development? *Key Issues in Development*. D. Kingsbury. Basingstoke, Palgrave: 22–44.

Rosser, A. (2007). The transitional support program in Timor Leste *Aid that works: successful development in fragile states*. J. Manor. Washington DC, World Bank: 59–84.

Rosser, A. (2008). Rebuilding governance in failed states: an illustration from Timor Leste. *Governance and the Depoliticisation of Development*. R. Robison and W. Hout. London, Routledge.

Scambary, J. (2006). A survey of gangs and youth groups in Dili, Timor-Leste. Dili, A report commissioned by AusAID.

Scambary, J. (2007). Disaffected groups and Social movements in East Timor.

Scambary, J. (2011). Anatomy of a conflict: the 2006–7 communal violence in East Timor. *Security, Development and Nation-Building in Timor-Leste: A cross-sectoral assessment*. V. Harris and A. Goldsmith. London and New York, Routledge.

Scambary, J. (2013). Informal security groups and social movements. *The Politics of Timor-Leste: Democratic consolidation after intervention*. M. Leach and D. Kingsbury. Ithaca, New York, Cornell University.

Schuurman, F. (1993). *Beyond the Impasse: New directions in development theory*. London, Zed Books.

Scott, D. (2005). *Last flight out of Dili: Memoirs of an accidental activist in the triumph of East Timor*. Melbourne, Pluto Press.

Seekings, J. (1996). "The "Lost generation": South Africa's "youth problem" in the early 1990's." *Transformation* 29: 103–125.

Seligson, M. (2003). Inequality in a Global perspective: directions for further research. *Development and Under-development: The political economy of global inequality*. M. Seligson and J. Passe-Smith. Boulder, Colorado, Lynne Rienner Publishers: 465–482.

Sen, A. (1999). *Development as Freedom*. Oxford & New York, Oxford University Press.

Sengstock, S. (2008). Reinado to live on as vivid figure in Timor folklore. *Canberra Times*. Canberra.

SEPI (2010). *Law Against Domestic Violence*. Dili, Secreatary of State for Promotion of Equality.

Shah, R. (2012). "Goodbye conflict, hello development? Curriculum reform in Timor-Leste." *International journal of educational development* 32: 31–38.

Silva, K. (2011). "Foho versus Dili: The political role of place in East Timor national imagination." *REALIS* 1(2): 144–165.

Simonsen, S. G. (2006). "The Authoritarian Temptation in East Timor." *Asian Survey* XLVI(4): 575–596.

Smillie, I. and L. Minear (2004). *The Charity of Nations: humanitarian action in a calculating world*. Bloomfield CT, Kumarian Press.

Soares, D. (2007). Engaging Young People in decision making in Timor Leste. Social Sciences. Melbourne, Victoria University.

SSYS & UNICEF (2005). National Youth Survey Dili, Secretary of State for Youth and Sport.

Stiglitz, J. E. (2002). *Globalization and its discontents*. New York & London, WW Norton & Co.

Sword Gusmao, K. (2003). *A Woman of Independence*. Sydney, Macmillan.

Taudevin, L. (1999). *East Timor: too little too late*. Sydney, Duffy & Snellgrove.

Taylor-Leech, K. (2005). "The ecology of language reform in East Timor: a language rights perspective." *Studies in Languages & Culture of East Timor* 7: 13–35.

Taylor-Leech, K. (2012). "Timor-Leste: Multilingual education for all?" *Ellipsis, Journal of the Amercian Portuguese Studies Association* 10: 55–72.

Tchailoro, N. R. (2013). Metamorfoze ONG Timor-Leste. *Understanding Timor-Leste*. T.-L. S. Association. Paper presented at the Understanding Timor-Leste Conference, 15-16 July 2013, Dili.

Thatcher, P. (1988). The role of women in East Timorese society, Anthropology dept. Monash University: 160.

Thu, P. M., S. Scott, et al. (2007). "Gendered access to customary land in East Timor." *GeoJournal* 69(4): 239–255.

Traube, E. (1995). Colonialism and decolonisation. *East Timor at the Crossroads: the forging of a nation*. P. Carey and G. C. Bentley. New York, Social Science Reseach Council: 42–55.

Traube, E. (2007). "Unpaid wages: local narratives and the imagination of the nation." *The Asia Pacific Journal of Anthropology* 8(1): 9–25.

Trembath, A. and D. Grenfell (2007). *Mapping the pursuit of gender equality*. Melbourne, Globalism Institute, RMIT University.

Trindade, J. (2011). Lulik: The core of Timorese values. *Communicating new research on Timor-Leste Conference*. Dili, Swinburne Press.

Trindade, J. and C. Bryant (2007). Rethinking Timorese identity as a peacebuilding srattegy: The Lorosa'e – Loromuno conflict from a traditional perspective. Dili, European Union & GTZ: 60.

Trinidade, J. and C. Bryant (2007). Rethinking Timorese identity as a peacebuilding srattegy: The Lorosa'e – Loromuno conflict from a traditional perspective. Dili, European Union & GTZ: 60.

UN (2005). United Nations Millennium Project Taskforce on Education and Gender Equality.

UNDP (2006). Path out of Poverty: Integrated Rural Development, Human Development Report 2006 Timor Leste. Dili: 2006.

UNDP (2013). The Rise of the South: Human progress in a diverse world. *Human Development Report*.

UNICEF (2006). Speak nicely to me: a study on practices and attitudes about discipline of children in Timor-Leste. Dili: 108.

van Schoor, V. (2005). Reviving Health Care. *Postconflict Development: Meeting new challenges.* G. Junne and W. Verkoren. Boulder, London, Lynne Rienner.

Victorino-Soriano, C. (2004). Obstacles to the effective participation of women in adult education program: Focus on social-cultural factors. Dili, Oxfam: 57.

Walsh, P. (2006). *Toward a new Timor-Leste: the shared responsibility of religious institutions.* Timor Leste Inter-Faith Conference, Baucau.

Wayte, K., A. B. Zwi, et al. (2008). "Conflict and Development: Challenges in responding to sexual and reproductive health needs in Timor Leste." *Reproductive Health Matters* 16(31): 83–92.

White, H. (2001). "Will the New Aid Agenda help promote poverty reduction?" *Journal of International Development* 13: 1057–1070.

Wigglesworth, A. (2006). Partnership in Crisis: Lessons from East Timor. *Aid and Conflict.* M. Clarke. New York, Nova Science Publishers.

Wigglesworth, A. (2007). Young people in rural development. *East Timor beyond Independence.* D. Kingsbury and M. Leach. Clayton, Monash University Press: 51–63.

Wigglesworth, A. (2008). Timor Leste Civil Society Analysis: Report of an in-country review and consultation for strengthening civil society. Canberra, Australian Council for International Development.

Wigglesworth, A. (2009). 'Young Women and gender dimensions of change in Timorese civil society'. *Understanding Timor Leste.* M Leach et al. Melbourne, Swinburne Press: 242-7.

Wigglesworth, A. (2012). "Dreaming of a different life: Steps towards democracy and equality in Timor-Leste." *Ellipsis, Journal of the American Portuguese Studies Association* 10: 35–53.

Wigglesworth, A. (2013a). "The Growth of Civil Society in Timor-Leste: Three Moments of Activism." *Journal of Contemporary Asia* 43(1): 51–74.

Wigglesworth, A. (2013b). "Community Leadership and Gender Equality: Experiences of Representation in Local Governance in Timor-Leste." *Asian Politics and Policy* 5(4): 567–584.

Wigglesworth, A. and A. B. dos Santos (forthcoming 2016). 'Customary values and global influences in youth attitudes to gender and violence in Timor-Leste'. *Proceedings of the Timor Leste Studies Association Conference 9-10 July 2015.*

Wigglesworth, A., S. Niner, et al. (2015). "Attitudes and perceptions of young men towards gender equality and violence in Timor-Leste." *Journal of International Women's Studies* 16(2).

Wigglesworth, A. and A. Soares (2006). Evaluation of FONGTIL. Dili, NGO Forum.

Williams, S. H. (2011). "Democracy, Gender Equality and Customary Law: Constitutionalizing internal cultural disruption." *Indiana Journal of Global Legal Studies* 18(1): 65–85.

World Bank (2003). Timor-Leste Education – The Way Forward. A Summary Report. Dili, World Bank: 36.

World Bank (2005). Implementation Completion Report on a proposed Trust Fund grant in the amount of US $16.5 million to Timor Leste for the Community Empowerment and Local Governance Project, Environment and Social Development Sector Unit, East Asia and Pacific Region, World Bank.

World Bank (2005). World Bank Country Assistance Strategy for Timor Leste FY 06–08. Dili.

World Bank (2013). Jobs. *World Development Report.*

World Bank and ADB (2005). Trust Fund for East Timor: Report of the Trustee and Proposed Work Program May 2005 – April 2006. Dili, World Bank.